Swift, Silent, and Deadly

Swift, Silent, and Deadly

*Marine Amphibious Reconnaissance
in the Pacific, 1942–1945*

Bruce F. Meyers

Naval Institute Press
Annapolis, Maryland

Naval Institute Press
291 Wood Road
Annapolis, MD 21402

Library of Congress Cataloging-in-Publication Data
Meyers, Bruce F., 1925–
        Swift, silent, and deadly : Marine amphibious reconnaissance in
the Pacific, 1942–1945 / Bruce F. Meyers.
        p. cm.
        Includes bibliographical references and index.
        ISBN 1-59114-484-1 (alk. paper)
        1. World War, 1939–1945—Campaigns—Oceania. 2. United
States. Marine Corps—History—World War, 1939–1945. 3. World War,
1939–1945—Reconnaissance operations, American. 4. World War,
1939–1945—Amphibious operations. 5. World War, 1939–1945—Naval
operations, American. I. Title.
        D767.9.M42 2004
        940.54'5—dc22

                                            2003023313

Printed in the United States of America on acid-free paper ∞
11 10 09 08 07 06 05 04   9 8 7 6 5 4 3 2
First printing

Many books about special operations are dedicated to the brave men who risked danger on distant missions. Instead, this book is dedicated to the marine recon wife. She must stay behind, encouraging and supportive, well aware of the dangers her recon marine must face. Each of us know a score, with names like Charlotte, Nancy, Polly, and Sue.

In my case, I add a special dedication to my wife of fifty-five years, Jo, whose encouragement, wit, support, and stoicism when tragedy was at hand have been my constant companion. No one could ask for a better partner for life's endeavors.

Contents

Foreword

The Marine Corps has, for the 228 years of its existence, fought our country's battles around the globe. Equally adept on land, on the sea, and, for the last 81 years, in the air, Marines have proven to be proficient, adaptive, and resourceful. Americans know that Marines are the nation's premier expeditionary force in readiness and that they are invariably successful in all they do.

This book is the story of amphibious reconnaissance, how it began, how it developed, and how, during World War II, it became the instrument of our national military capability, preceding every major amphibious landing in the Pacific. Marines and their accompanying Navy corpsmen were regularly inserted behind enemy lines, well in advance of an operation, to obtain naval intelligence on beach hydrography, on terrain, and particularly on the enemy and his fortifications. Returning with this information permitted successful prosecution of each and every campaign in which they were used. Reconnaissance Marines were involved in nearly two hundred landings, most of which occurred at night, the Marines coming ashore either in rubber boats or swimming in from landing craft, submarines, PT boats, seaplanes (PBYs), and Navy high-speed destroyer transports (APDs). Other important missions that reconnaissance Marines conducted include the training and employment of the Alaska Scouts at Attu and Kiska in the Aleutians and training and working with the Army Alamo Scouts in the Southwest Pacific in New Guinea and the Philippines.

Marine reconnaissance units were formed before what we now call "special-ops"—special operations. Formed in December 1941 at Quantico, Virginia, these units were organized and operating before the establishment of OSS (the Office of Strategic Services—June 1942), before UDT (underwater demolition teams—May 1943), before Army Special Forces (antecedent to the Green Berets—November 1942), and before the Air Commandos (1 October 1943).

Marines have a long history of adaptation to diverse combat situations. One of the first examples of this adaptive ability came in the Florida swamps in May 1836, when the Marines of our fifth commandant, Archibald Henderson, worked with friendly Creek Indians to scout ahead and to the flanks of his troops. During World War I, the 5th and 6th Marines used patrols adept at field craft and marksmanship to penetrate German lines. They sniped unsuspecting German troops and returned with invaluable intelligence from "behind the lines." In the period between the world wars, Marine leaders such as "Chesty" Puller, Herman Hanneken, and William Button displayed great ingenuity in their patrol actions behind enemy lines. This was later chronicled in the Corps's key publication of the era, *The Small Wars Manual.* And it was in the late 1920s and mid-1930s that Navy admirals and Marine generals began to institutionalize the conduct of amphibious landings. During this period, experimentation occurred when reconnaissance patrols were inserted onto "enemy" beaches at Vieques in Puerto Rico during fleet landing exercises. It became apparent to Maj. Gen. Holland M. "Howlin Mad" Smith that the Marines needed units specially trained and equipped to land behind enemy lines. This led to the formation of the initial Observer Group at Quantico in December 1941.

My father, (then) Capt. James L. Jones, took command of these men and initially formed an amphibious reconnaissance company, later expanding it to the Amphibious Reconnaissance Battalion. This is the story of that battalion and other similar units that performed brilliantly in conducting amphibious reconnaissance from Guadalcanal and the Solomons in 1942–43, to the capture of Iwo Jima and Okinawa in 1945, and all the major campaigns in between. And as it is with all elite units, these men became very close—the memories of the camaraderie between my father and his officers and men who shared these combat experiences remain with me to this day.

This reconnaissance story is told by Col. Bruce Meyers, USMC, who began his career as a young lieutenant commanding a combat swimming platoon at the end of World War II. During this time, he worked with Col. Herman Hanneken, one of the commanders in the Banana Wars. After commanding a rifle company in Korea, Colonel Meyers worked as Brig. Gen. "Chesty" (Lewis B.) Puller's reconnaissance officer. While commanding the reconnaissance school at Coronado, he went through UDT SCUBA School and learned about parachutes and parachuting. His ideas on improving reconnaissance techniques were implemented by our twentieth commandant, Gen. Lemuel C. Shepherd, leading to the formation of 1st Force Reconnaissance Company, the dedicated deep-reconnaissance agency of the Marine Corps. This unit was to become the modern-day descendant of my father's Amphibious Reconnaissance Battalion. As its first commanding officer, Colonel Meyers helped develop new techniques for entry, from jets launched from aircraft carriers, to high altitude/low opening (HALO) parachute jumps, to exiting and locking back in to submerged submarines, to name a few. He writes with the experience of my father's generation, having launched on a number of night landings by rubber boat from the sea-swept deck of a hastily submerging submarine. As a combat swimmer and diver, he has swum the long distances to objective beaches. His initial 1st Force Recon Company was expanded and, during the height of the Vietnam War, six such force recon companies were in existence. Grenada and both wars in Iraq again proved the mettle of these young reconnaissance Marines and corpsmen.

This is the story of those World War II reconnaissance Marines, fifty-plus of whom survive to this day. Colonel Meyers has used the personal experiences of those Marines whenever possible. This is the story of "the ancestors" of our current generation of reconnaissance Marines.

General James L. Jones, Jr., USMC
Supreme Allied Commander, Europe/
Commander, U.S. European Command
32d Commandant of the Marine Corps

Acknowledgments

In researching for the writing of a history of this scope (all reconnaissance activities in the Pacific theater), one turns first to those who served in the campaigns of which one writes. In addition, I was ably helped by the Historical and Museums Division at Headquarters Marine Corps and the Gray Research Center at Quantico, Virginia. The excellent treatises and accounts of World War II actions helped round out this research. Among others, these included the works of Col. Joseph Alexander, Lt. Col. Jon Hoffman, Chaplain Ray Stubbe, Lt. Col. Michael Lanning, Rear Adm. Samuel Eliot Morison, and the several authors of the five-volume set of U.S. Marine Operations in the Pacific.

Particularly helpful in researching and writing this book were Lt. Gen. Lewis B. "Chesty" Puller, Maj. Gen. Kenneth Houghton, Brig. Gen. Russell Corey, Brig. Gen. Regan Fuller, Col. Clay Boyd, Col. Edward L. Katzenbach Jr. (later deputy assistant secretary of defense), Col. Leo B. Shinn, Col. Merwyn Silverthorn, Col. Anthony "Cold Steel" Walker, Maj. John D. Bradbeer, Capt. Charles "Pat" Patrick, Lt. Sam Lanford, Sgt. Jim Burns, Sgt. Wayne Pilny, Sgt. Clete Peacock, Cpl. John Schiller, PFC Nelson Donley, PFC Donald McNeese, and PFC John Seborn.

As CO 1st Force Recon Company, I worked with the legendary Rear. Adm. Draper Kaufman, who shared with me details of his many UDT operations. In like manner, my friend Col. Sherm Wilkins, USAF (Ret.), ensured that my comments regarding the Army Air Corps were accurate. My friend Capt. Dan Scarborough (skipper of two submarines) obtained formerly secret histories of all WORLD WAR II submarine operations and kept me on track regarding submarines. My neighbor, former Navy lieutenant commander Bill Burke, did wonders with photo restoration.

Marine Corps historians who were particularly helpful include Directors Brig. Gen. Ed Simmons and Col. John Ripley, Historians of the Marine Corps, Benis Frank, and, later, Charles Melson, and his photo curator Lena Kaljot, and historian and author Don Shaw. Carey Strong and Belinda Kelly at Gray Research Center at the Marine Corps University gave me able tutelage and help.

Offering encouragement, friendship, and helpful anecdotal material was Charlotte Jones, widow of Maj. Jim Jones Sr., CO VAC Amphib Recon Battalion, who was the father of Gen. James Jones, our immediate past commandant of the Marine Corps, currently serving as supreme allied commander Europe and commander U.S. European Command.

Last, I wish to thank the able staff at the Naval Institute Press: Eric Mills, Susan Artigiani, Kristin Wye-Rodney, Sara Sprinkle, and Donna Doyle. Thanks for the professionalism of my copy editor, Karin Kaufman. She made this a better book.

In conclusion, when one lists a number of people who helped, one may inadvertently leave out others who helped equally. To them I apologize and ask them to consider themselves included.

Introduction

During the early morning darkness, the sleek black hull of the submarine *Nautilus* broke the surface of the central Pacific, in the midst of the Gilbert Islands. It was off the five-islet coral atoll of Apamama, seventy-six miles due south of Tarawa. Six of the Marines Corps's ten-man rubber boats had been stowed in the after part of the superstructure, astern and below the conning tower. Back at Pearl Harbor, the crew of *Nautilus* had rigged air hoses and were eager to try a new method of launching. Instead of lowering the boats over the side then loading, they opted to do a "wet-deck" launch. (In such a launch, marines inflate and load their boats on the after-deck, or fantail, of the submarine, and the submarine submerges from beneath them.) Positioning the boats on the fantail, they inflated the air hoses. The skipper, Cdr. Bill Irwin, gave the order to clear the bridge, and *Nautilus* moved ahead slowly as he took it down, the marines in their boats sited in pairs on the after-deck. This was the first recorded combat use of a wet-deck launch of reconnaissance (recon) marines in the Pacific. Debarkation went well.

Capt. Jim Jones and the bulk of his sixty-eight marines and corpsmen (Navy medical personnel assigned to the marines) plus ten EOD engineers and supernumeraries had been riding *Nautilus* since early November 1943. They were en route to just off the surf line. A nasty, three-knot cross-current sea and frequent rain squalls, in addition to the darkness, made the trip hazardous and longer than expected. Outboard motors quit in the vicious surf. Yet all of the marines made it, landing on the very western tip of the atoll, and began their reconnaissance and subsequent seizure of the tiny islets. Their mission, top secret until declassified after the war, was part of the strategic plan for assault of the Japanese bases throughout the Pacific. The task force commander wished to ensure security for the main Marine landing at Tarawa. Apamama, like most of the other groups of small islets called atolls, was just one more atoll in the "family" of atolls called the Gilberts.

With linguistic help from the Australian scout officer, Lt. George Hard, a former Coastwatcher who landed with their patrol, they sought information from the natives. The twenty-five Japanese troops on the atoll were overcome with the assistance of naval gunfire from *Nautilus* and, later, the destroyer *Gansevoort* (DD-608), Lt. Cdr. J. M. Steinbeck commanding.

Improvisation being the recon unit's hallmark, mattress covers were sewn together into two-by-sixteen-foot canvas strips and were used for two purposes: (1) as a "code" for the *Nautilus* (e.g., two vertical parallel mattress covers meant "situation in hand," no requirements for ammo, etc.) and (2) as panels to identify the front lines for the DD's later naval gunfire support (the standard-issue air panels were much smaller and virtually invisible from any distance at sea). The five islets were rapidly secured by these recon marines, and the main landings on Tarawa and Makin were thus made more secure from outside Japanese influence.

Although their original mission was to "scout" for Japanese, as one of the amphibious (amphib) recon marines later stated, "We had to stay there for five days, and there wasn't room for the Japs and us too." A number of the Japanese defense forces were killed by the recon marines, some were killed by naval gunfire, and the remainder committed suicide before the Marines' final assault. The first amphib recon casualty of the war, PFC William D. Miller, was killed in the initial assault on the Japanese garrison. Another marine died of wounds after being evacuated aboard ship. Later, the 3d Battalion, 6th Marines (from the 2d Marine Division on Tarawa) landed at Apamama and set up a defensive perimeter for the projected airfield.

Marines assigned to scout or recon a planned or potential landing site performed more than two hundred such landings, the majority during darkness. They came in from submarines, patrol torpedo boats, Catalina flying boats, and high-speed destroyer-transports. Most recons were clandestine, with marines, faces darkened, carrying minimal weapons, swimming or coming in by rubber boat through the surf. Frequently, when the beach was a tasked objective for the larger amphibious landing to follow, the recon marines would be accompanied by underwater demolition teams (UDTs). These brave Marine and Navy personnel replicated such missions throughout the Pacific from 1942 to 1945, up through the final landings on Japanese soil (for example, Iwo Jima and Okinawa).

This is the story of these diverse groups whose landings on enemy beaches was swift, silent, and deadly. Attempting to avoid detection at all costs, their mission was not to initiate combat, as their fellow marines would do in the follow-on assault landings. Their task was to obtain intelligence. They would measure water depths, chart coral heads, evaluate the beaches, and look for exits off the beaches for their landing compatriots. Of prime importance, they took photographs and soil samples, always attempting to locate enemy units and weapons. In short, they obtained all of the information possible on a potential beach or landing area.

Great progress had been made in acquisition of pre–D-day intelligence, for this and all future Pacific D days, through aerial and periscope (submarine) photography, however, cloud cover, enemy fire, and lack of accurate charts and maps all dictated that, for the landing force commander to have the essential information he required, the personal, on-the-spot, "down and dirty" recon had to be done by these marines. In writing their story, I have used operation orders once classified secret and top secret that have been now declassified as well as interviewed scores of the participants. As a young lieutenant in World War II, I commanded a combat swimming platoon just before the end of the war. I had the opportunity of working with these participants in the surf and from the deck of submarines, but I did not take part in any of the operations about which I write. As we move further in time from World War II, I feel it is important to tell the story of these missions and share the unique experiences of the recon marines.

It is equally important to tell the story of marine reconnaissance. As this book is being written, U.S. forces are again in combat, operating behind enemy lines in Afghanistan and Iraq.

Our services now identify these small groups of men who operate frequently behind enemy lines—the Army's Special Forces and Delta Force, the Navy Seals, and, for the Corps, Force Reconnaissance—as "special operations qualified." Although more than four hundred miles from the Persian Gulf, these naval and marine forces are deployed inland, performing clandestine missions that replicate many of the World War II missions of their service ancestors—Corps recon and Navy UDT.

As a marine officer with twenty-eight years of infantry and reconnaissance service, I initially approached the subject of this book with some preconceived expectations about amphibious reconnaissance in the Pacific theater. I was wrong.

I had always considered that the Amphibious Reconnaissance Battalion of the V Amphibious Corps was about the only unit doing amphibious reconnaissance, but I found that a considerable number of amphib recons were performed by Marine division personnel such as Scouts and Snipers (an element in the Marine division headquarters battalion that later became the recon companies), elements of the Raider battalions, the Parachute battalions, Allied units such as the Coastwatchers, and U.S. Army units such as the Alaska Scouts in the Aleutians and the Army, Navy, and Marine personnel in the Alamo Scouts in the Southwest Pacific.

I had also been under the impression that the Aleutian campaign was strictly an Army affair and was surprised to find that Maj. Gen. Holland M. "Howlin' Mad" Smith and a number of his Marine officer staff (including Capt. James Logan Jones) had been attached to the assault force as advisers. Earlier they had helped train the Army assault unit—Amphibious Training Force 9, a provisional corps composed of U.S. Army and Canadian assault units. Some advisers were attached to U.S. Army units. M.Gy. Sgt. Pat Patrick trained and later landed with the Canadian Brigade (Winnipeg Grenadiers) in their assault on Kiska.

Most people believe that UDTs have always been strictly Navy units, but such was not the case until March 1944. They were provisional units that were manned by not only Navy personnel but also Marine and Army demolitionists. It was not until after the Marshall Island campaign in late 1943 that the Navy was given control of such missions and organized the first permanent UDTs.

In writing this history of amphibious reconnaissance in the Pacific, of necessity I have had to paint the background of the main assault landings. This is done only to put the recon units' participation in perspective. I have attempted to avoid in-depth detail, commanders' names, small units' identifications or designations, and so forth on the main landings and, instead, I have attempted to concentrate primarily on the reconnaissance activities. For those students of military history who wish more depth with respect to the major unit participants, I suggest histories of World War II that cover these types of details. Rear Adm. Samuel Eliot Morison's fifteen-volume set is one of the best, and the official Marine Corps history, a five-volume set, is far more comprehensive than this book. Other suggested books include Col. Joseph Alexander's *Storm Landings,* Lt. Col. Jon Hoffman's *Once a Legend* (on Col. "Red" Mike Edson), and Lance Zedric's *Silent Warriors of World War II.*

To my knowledge, there has been no attempt until now to encapsulate a complete overview, a compendium if you will, of the myriad reconnaissance operations conducted by a number of diverse units who were involved in what we call amphibious reconnaissance.

The term "special operations," or "spec-ops," is often used in the press, in ward rooms and squadron ready rooms, and, of course, in war college classrooms. It has become the favorite catchword.

Marine Corps specialized reconnaissance units started in the Corps in the early 1930s, five years before the Army began to take notice—years before Special Forces and the Green Berets and, yes, years before the formation of the Office of Strategic Services (OSS). The Corps was carrying out hydrographic recon behind the lines on beaches years before the Navy formed its UDTs and decades before the SEALs came into existence. The Corps, early on, perceived the need for critical intelligence on potential operating areas. We are thankful that we had visionaries such as Lt. Col. Pete Ellis, between World War I and World War II in the Pacific, and Maj. Jim Jones, founder of marine amphibious recon in World War II. Let's go back and see how it started.

Swift, Silent, and Deadly

1

In the Beginning

Marines aboard Navy ships began to develop amphibious tactics in the late 1920s in the Caribbean. The overall lessons learned in these early landings coalesced into what eventually became the Fleet Marine Force, or FMF, an amalgamation of all of the different types of units considered necessary for a Marine force to project itself ashore for the seizure of littoral areas of the world.

Beginning in 1934, shortly after the formation of the Fleet Marine Force, the commander in chief of the U.S. Fleet approved a general plan for training the force for landing operations with the fleet. Planning between the U.S. Fleet and the Marine Corps began immediately, and the Caribbean was again designated as the site for the first in a series of fleet landing exercises, in military vernacular called FLEXs. Culebra, an island just north of Vieques, off the eastern coast of Puerto Rico, was chosen as the objective for these landings. This was prior to the establishment of the Corps's first division-sized organization.

The battleships *Arkansas* and *Wyoming* and the transport *Antares* carried the bulk of the troops. The ships' fifty-foot whaleboats were used to land the troops. Biplanes provided smoke screens, and in the initial landings, marines came down cargo nets hung over the sides of the transporting vessels. Ramps over the bows of the whaleboats were used with an A-frame to land artillery pieces and vehicles.[1]

I describe the anachronistic methods of some of our first landing exercises to provide the reader with the contrast and some insight into the rapid development which occurred during the next seven years. This culminated in the United States' first major

Pacific amphibious (amphib) combat operation of World War II, the 1st Marine Division's landing on Guadalcanal in the Solomon Islands of the South Pacific in August 1942.

Each year, fleet landing exercises were conducted with improvements and modifications. By 1936, the Fleet Marine Force Headquarters had moved to San Diego, where similar landing exercises were being done with the 2d Marine Brigade, another regimental-size unit (of the 6th Marines), at San Clemente Island off San Diego.[2]

In 1938, submarines began to be used for the landing of small parties of marines onto enemy beaches for reconnaissance purposes. Four submarines from SubRon-11 (Submarine Squadron 11) participated, landing recon teams from each of the submarines involved. Surfacing at night, aircraft-type rubber boats were inflated and launched over the side and marines landed and conducted their missions. The after-action report on this 1938 FLEX had an annex report (a compendium providing details on activities) from Company F, 5th Marines which described these rubber-boat missions from *S-47* and their subsequent beach reconnaissance.[3]

In 1941, the Marines for the first time used modified World War I–vintage destroyers as their means of transport. Mothballed since 1922, the Navy converted six "four-stackers," removing two of the four boilers and two of their stacks; spaces gained were turned into troop and cargo areas. These ships were redesignated "high-speed destroyer transports" (APDs). Early on in World War II, destroyer escort (DE) hulls were substituted for the converted four-stackers and became a newer, faster, and more modern class of APDs, which were later extensively used by recon marines and accompanying UDTs.[4]

At first, amphib recon teams landed by rubber boat, paddling initially but later adding outboard motors, launched from these first APDs. Subsequently, "Higgins boats" or other types of modified landing craft were used to tow the rubber boats closer to the target beach, where they would cast off and go in by outboard motor or paddling.

The U.S. Fleet and Fleet Marine Force began to gather and publish the lessons learned from the fleet landing exercises and thus was born FTP (fleet training publication) 167, *Landing Operations Doctrine*. Amphibious reconnaissance missions covered in FTP 167 were expanded to include location of enemy defensive positions, including troop strengths, weapons, obstacles and defenses, and the character of the surf, beach, and terrain inland, including the ever-important beach exits to permit the landing force to get off the beaches. The above mission requirements were included in the *Landing Force Manual* as a "directed effort by personnel landed from seaward by any means to collect the information on a coastal area required for the planning and conduct of amphibious operations." This later was further refined to include "a landing conducted by minor elements, involving stealth rather than force of arms for the purpose of securing information, followed by a planned withdrawal."[5]

2

The Units

Marine Corps intelligence assets during World War II included amphibious reconnaissance units, organized as such; Marine division organic units that participated in amphibious reconnaissance; and specialized units such as the Marine Raiders and the Paramarines. Adding to the complexity of amphibious intelligence, Allied units and units from other U.S. services, the Navy in particular, were also involved.

The Observer Group

In December 1941, a small group of Army and twenty-two Marine Corps officers and noncommissioned officers (NCOs) were gathered from various intelligence sections from both services and assembled in Quantico, Virginia. Collectively, they were called the Observer Group. The group was formed on order of Maj. Gen. Holland M. "Howlin Mad" Smith, then commanding general (CG) of the Amphibious Corps, Atlantic Fleet, headquartered at Quantico. Marines were pooled from the 5th Marines' battalion intelligence sections (S-2), regimental intelligence (then the R-2), and Division Intelligence Section (G-2 Sections) of the 1st Marine Division. The Observer Group became the first Marine Corps unit whose specific mission was amphibious reconnaissance.[1]

The Observer Group began experimentation in methodology and equipment for launching reconnaissance from the sea. Sgt. Thomas L. Curtis was selected from the Observer Group and sent to England, where he trained with the Royal Marines. He later transferred to OSS, where he served with distinction.[2] Rubber boats became the recon boat of choice, although tests and trials were also done using kayaks and folding canvas boats.

Guiding criteria demanded that such craft would have to fit through the rather small hatches of fleet submarines. At the same time, various weapons were tried. The Marines were taught knife fighting and escape techniques by British Commando instructor Lt. Col. William E. Fairbairn, formerly of the Shanghai Municipal Police, who had taught knife and club fighting to the 4th Marines in Shanghai (see "Fairbairn-Sykes" in the glossary). About this time, the Observer Group was sent to the FBI School, which was on the base at Quantico. For two weeks FBI agents taught them "the rudiments of ju-jitsu, pistol shooting from the hip, [and] firing the TMSG (Thompson sub-machine gun.)"[3]

The Observer Group was initially a joint Army and Navy organization, the plan being for the Army and the Marine Corps to make landings on North Africa. Training was done on the Potomac and Chesapeake Rivers. Submarine work was done at New London, Connecticut. Later, they carried out exercises on both the Atlantic and Caribbean. Capt. James Logan Jones Sr., who was on General Smith's staff, was assigned to G-2 on the Amphibious Corps staff. Jones had lived overseas in Europe and North Africa before the war and, speaking several languages, was a natural fit for intelligence. His brother, Maj. William K. Jones (later a lieutenant general), convinced him to transfer his Army commission for a Marine commission. The Corps gained greatly by that transfer.

The Observer Group was first led by the Army's 1st Lt. Loyd Peddicord Jr. It began operating under the staff supervision of the Amphib Corps, Atlantic Fleet G-2, Lt. Col. Louis Ely, USA. Much of the early recon instruction was taught by the Marine's Plt. Sgt. Russell Corey. The group's submarine training was done in June 1942 at the submarine school in New London, Connecticut. Corey took the Observer Group (twenty marines, one soldier) for this hands-on work at sea aboard fleet submarines and in the tower for instruction in the Momsen lung.[4]

While those in the Observer Group was honing their operational skills, the Amphib Corps intelligence officers were working out the tactical utilization of amphibious reconnaissance. They began to develop the how, when, and where of amphib recons.

In September 1942, the Observer Group was disbanded at Quantico. The Army component went to North Africa, as had been planned, while the Marine component (two officers and twenty enlisted) was sent to Camp Elliot, just northeast of San Diego. In January 1943, the Observer Group became the nucleus forming the first amphibious reconnaissance company, under command of Capt. James Logan Jones Sr.

Amphibious Reconnaissance Company, Amphibious Corps, Pacific Fleet

This initial amphibious reconnaissance company, consisting of six officers and ninety-two enlisted, was organized with a headquarters platoon and four reconnaissance platoons. Each platoon was commanded by a lieutenant and consisted of two six-man squads. The platoons were thus tailored, with equipment, to embark in either two ten-man rubber boats or three seven-man boats.

During the next nine months in the Camp Elliot/Camp Pendleton area, they continued training, honing scouting and patrolling techniques and becoming proficient with their rubber boats in the heavy Pacific surf. Here they operated from both submarines and APDs. Additionally, the company made a training film, *The Amphibious Reconnaissance Patrol* (which, interestingly, is still used today in amphib recon training). They passed their amphib recon skills on to the Army, training two Army units in amphibious reconnaissance. These Army units, the Alaska Scouts, performed well in the taking of Attu and Kiska in the Aleutian campaign. Later, in the Army landing on Kwajalein, one of these same, Marine-trained, Army amphib recon units was cited for its excellent performance. In August 1943, a further titular change was made, and the company became the Amphibious Reconnaissance Company, V (Fifth) Amphibious Corps (VAC), Pacific Fleet. The following month, the company shipped out to Hawaii, where they took up their wartime quarters at Camp Catlin on Oahu, there adding one additional recon platoon (for a total of five). On 16 September 1943, Captain Jones, as the only marine, boarded the large mine-laying submarine *Nautilus* (SS-168) for a month-long patrol, during which he assisted in periscope recons of Tarawa, Kuma, Butaritari, Makin, and Apamama Atolls. The *Nautilus* returned on 16 October 1943, and briefings were begun to prepare the company for their first mission. *Nautilus* departed Pearl Harbor on 8 November, bound for Tarawa and, later, Apamama Atoll, some seventy-six miles due south of Tarawa. The company headquarters and three platoons participated in this operation, which is more fully described in chapter 6.

Amphibious Reconnaissance Battalion, VAC

By April 1944, as a result of combat experience, casualties, and increasing operational commitments, the Amphibious Reconnaissance Company, VAC was expanded, redesignated, and reorganized into the Amphibious Reconnaissance Battalion. It became a two-recon company (Companies A and B), one headquarters company, 303 Marine Battalion. This battalion was amalgamated and redesignated in April 1944 as Amphibious Reconnaissance Battalion, FMF, retaining this name until its disbandment at the end of the war on 24 September 1945.[5]

Marine Division's Scouts and Snipers

When the first two Marine divisions were formed in 1941, each regiment had a scout and sniper platoon in the regimental headquarters and service company. In 1944, these were amalgamated later into a division reconnaissance company of 5 officers and 122 enlisted located in the Division Headquarters Battalion. Augmentation for these newly redesignated reconnaissance companies (born from the Scouts and Snipers) came from the recently disbanded Raider and Parachute battalions.[6] Transport was by foot or jeep on land and by rubber boat when embarked. These companies were used in a variety of tasks and, on occasion in severe combat, were used as "spare" rifle companies (e.g., 4th Marine Division Scout Company under Capt. Edward L. Katzenbach Jr. was so used in the landings on Eniwetok and Parry Island in the western Marshalls)(see chap. 7).[7] As a result of their strong training in scouting and patrolling, they were well suited to occasional mopping-up operations following major Marine units' landings. (*Author's note:* Some reconnaissance purists feel that such utilization was a misuse of reconnaissance assets, however, on balance, in combat, when a division or regimental commander is short of assets, he will use any unit that can help accomplish the mission. I know that I would have considered such years later in Vietnam, as others of my peers did. Fortunately, in Vietnam I never had to use recon assets as infantry.) These division recon companies were used primarily when a particular mission within the Marine division involved specialized reconnaissance. An example of such use is described in chapter 5 on Guadalcanal in the Solomons.

Other Service and Foreign Reconnaissance Agencies and Units

Naval Commando Demolition Units

In 1942, the Army and the Navy jointly established the Amphibious Scout and Raider School at Fort Pierce, Florida, to train individual soldiers, sailors, and marines in demolitions, raids, and patrols.[8] Trained by Lt. Cdr. Phil H. Bucklew and, later, Lt. Draper L. Kaufman, USN, these naval commando demolition units (NCDUs) were first employed in Operation Torch in the invasion of North Africa in 1942. Later, in May 1943, Kaufman expanded the syllabus and established a more Navy-oriented school for underwater demolition. Initially near the Fort Pierce Amphibious Scouts and Raiders School, again, however, it was jointly manned by the Army and Marines in addition to naval personnel. Following the near-disaster on the reefs at Tarawa in November 1943, Read Adm. Richmond Kelly Turner, the Navy's "amphibious admiral," directed the formation of nine UDT teams and establishment of the Navy Experimental and Tactical Demolition Station on Waimanalo, Oahu, later moving to Kamaole, Maui, Hawaii. This became "Navy UDT" as we know it today (and was the birthing of what were later to be called SEALs).[9]

Navy Underwater Demolition Teams

UDT teams did not become solely a Navy mission until August 1944. Hydrographic reconnaissance was still shared with the Marines. The Corps performed the hydrographic recon from the one-fathom line in, to, and up onto the beach, and the UDT teams would do the deeper hydrographic recon, from the one-fathom line out, marking boat lanes as necessary and removing or marking underwater obstacles such as coral heads and shoals. Any necessary demolition missions in the approach and surf zones were done by UDT.[10] The UDT teams were organized with approximately sixteen officers and eighty men. There was one Marine officer and one Army officer as liaison with each team.[11] It became normal for the UDT assigned to a particular beach to ride the same APD that its counterpart amphibious reconnaissance unit was riding. As an example, during the Tinian operation (see chap. 8), eight boats were used for 1st Lt. Leo Shinn's B Company, VAC Amphib Recon Battalion, and two boats were used for Lt. Cdr. Draper Kaufman's UDT Team 5 for recon and hydrographic work on White Beaches 1 and 2.[12]

Alaska Scouts

The Army trained and organized a small (five hundred–plus) unit called the Alaska Scouts, spawned from the Alaska Territorial Guard (ATG). The Alaska Scouts were composed primarily of Alaskans, mostly fisherman and trappers, many of whom were natives (including Aleuts). Rugged and resourceful, these units quickly adapted well to Marine recon training in California. Returning to Alaska, they participated in the recapture of both Attu and Kiska in the Aleutian campaign. They reconnoitered for five days from the submarines *Narwhal* and *Nautilus* prior to the main landings on Attu. On 11 May 1943, each submarine landed about one hundred Alaska Scouts (including many Aleuts) near Holtz Bay. Finding the north coast unoccupied, they established a beachhead and began to move south and inland. Later on the afternoon of the same day, on the other (southern) side of Attu island, the Southern Landing Force put some four hundred troops from a recon troop on the southern-coast beach at Massacre Bay. Quickly moving north and inland, they intended to join up with the Northern Landing Force. The major battle with the Japanese defenders took place when the Japanese were "pincered" between these two landing forces. Following this, the landing force secured the entire island. As noted earlier, marine recon personnel accompanied the assault elements on these landings.[13]

Alamo Scouts

The Alamo Scouts were established in November 1943 by the Army's Lt. Gen. Walter Kreuger. This group's mission was much like that of its Marine counterparts: to scout and obtain intelligence

9

before the landings and seizure of major areas in the South Pacific. The Alamo Scouts established their own training syllabus and operated with great success in the Bismarck Archipelago and New Guinea. Later, they concluded their actions during World War II in seizure of Leyte in the Philippines. (An excellent in-depth resource on the Alamo Scouts can be found in Lance Q. Zedric's *Silent Warriors.*)

Coastwatchers

Established by the Australian Navy in 1939, the Coastwatchers were a small group of mostly Australian naval personnel organized by Cdr. Eric Feldt, RAN. Later, a few U.S. personnel were added. Jointly, they manned and operated a network of radio stations in islands occupied by the Japanese, principally in the Bismarcks and Solomons. Many of them were former traders, planters, prospectors, and island government officials. Most were intimately familiar with their assigned locales. They trained native residents to provide a network of intelligence throughout this area. They proved themselves invaluable in their alerts of impending Japanese shipping and aircraft en route to U.S. installations, aircraft, and ships, particularly at Guadalcanal and Bougainville. The Coastwatchers were later called the Allied Intelligence Bureau (AIB) or, sometimes, the Allied Intelligence Force (AIF). They were resupplied and supported by both Australian and U.S. forces using Catalina flying boats (PBYs), submarines, patrol torpedo boats (PTs), and APDs.[14] Interestingly, when I formed 1st Force Recon in 1957, establishment of up to nine coastwatching stations became one of the assigned mission capabilities of the Marine reconnaissance companies.[15]

Swift, Silent, and Deadly

tically blamed the Carlson raid for this rapid Japanese buildup in the Gilberts and staunchly felt, even after his retirement, that instead of incurring heavy Marine casualties in its agonizing seizure, Tarawa should have been bypassed.[4]

Strategically, Admirals King, Nimitz, and Spruance felt that retaking the Gilberts was essential for our continued movement westward toward the Marshalls. The code name for the capture of the Gilberts was Galvanic.[5] Plans called for the seizure of Tarawa, then the seizure of Makin. Apamama, some seventy-six miles south of Tarawa and believed to be minimally occupied, would follow Makin.

On 16 September 1943, Capt. Jim Jones of the Marines and Capt. D. L. Newman of the Army reported aboard the submarine *Nautilus* at the submarine base in Pearl Harbor. The sub's skipper, Cdr. William D. Irwin, met them at the gangway and took them to their quarters. They were to accompany *Nautilus* on its sixth war patrol.[6] Their mission: periscope reconnaissance of Tarawa, Kuma, Butaritari, Makin, and Apamama Atolls. Rear Adm. Richmond Kelly Turner, commanding the amphibious assault, wanted detailed photographic coverage of all of the beaches to be involved in retaking the Gilberts. Jones was able to personally view the beaches (via the periscope of *Nautilus*) at the site of his unit's next mission.

At the time, periscope photography was still in its infancy. A few sub skippers had made dramatic single shots of their sinkings, but what Admiral Turner and General Smith wanted were more detailed and definitively located photos of the beaches arranged in precise panoramic succession. These would show enemy machine-gun and antiboat gun emplacements and locations of terrain features. They could be used in conjunction with regular aerial photographs for more detailed photo interpretation. The Navy provided specially fabricated brackets (mechanical "shelves" attached to the periscope to hold cameras) and three types of cameras: (1) a large view camera, (2) a camera using medium-sized roll film, and (3) a miniature 35-mm camera. The lower sonar room was turned into a photo darkroom. Early on, it became apparent that the Navy cameras could not provide the detail that was needed. Making the task even more difficult was the tendency of the periscope to vibrate and the fact that periscopes only admit 35 percent of ambient light.

Fortuitously, the ship's exec, Lt. Cdr. Richard Lynch, was an avid amateur photographer. He had with him a medium-sized, single-lens reflex camera of German manufacture called a Primaflex. It took 2.25-by-2.25-inch negatives, which proved to be far superior to negatives from any of the Navy's cameras. Each photo of that camera's twelve-exposure roll was overlapped by 50 percent, which, as the photos were taken, was coordinated carefully with a chart of the island, giving the submarine's exact distance from each beach.[7]

Nautilus arrived back at Pearl on 16 October 1943, after eighteen days of periscope photography. The photos were a boon to the intelligence officers and were quickly reproduced and distributed in time for the respective invasions. All Navy submarines were subsequently retrofitted with specially designed brackets for periscope cameras. Calls went out for civilian donations or loans of the Primaflex cameras, and the problem was solved for future periscope photography.

Tarawa, November 1943

The D-day for Tarawa and Makin was 10 November; Apamama was to be on the twenty-first. Other than periscope photography, there was no recon prior to the landing on Tarawa, but the first unit to land at Betio on the Tarawa Atoll was the 2d Marine's Scout-Sniper Platoon, a recon-type unit. 1st Lt. William D. Hawkins's platoon, in basically a "assault scouting" role, secured the island ramp at the foot of one of the two long piers extending into the lagoon. The Scouts and Snipers continued to fight with distinction. The only other recon-type unit involved at Tarawa was the Scout-Sniper Platoon of the 8th Marines that worked with that regiment in their later assault. Lieutenant Hawkins was killed during this action and posthumously received the Congressional Medal of Honor.[8] Company D, 2d Tank Battalion, the division's Scout company, did work extensively in the seizure and occupation of other islands in the Tarawa Atoll, other than Betio, including Eita and an unnamed island between Bairiki and Betio. In addition, the adjacent atolls of Abaiang, Marakei, and Maianna were landed on to inspect for fortifications, supplies, or recent occupancy.

Makin, November 1943

The 4th Platoon, Amphibious Reconnaissance Company, VAC commanded by 1st Lt. Harvey C. Weeks's Marine platoon, was detached from VAC Amphib Recon Company for the Makin operation. Weeks's platoon was augmented with a rifle platoon and a machine-gun squad from the Army's 165th Infantry Regiment. This combined force was used to occupy Kotabu, a reef-fringed islet guarding the entrance to Makin Atoll's lagoon. Their landing was unopposed. Their occupation of Kotabu denied its use to the Japanese during the U.S. Army's later assault of Makin Island proper. Weeks's platoon was later used with the 165th Infantry, assisting in the mop-up on Butaritari. Makin was formally declared secure on 23 November 1943.[9] Weeks, interestingly, had been a practicing attorney, a Yale grad, before enlisting in the Marine Corps as a private. He was commissioned out of Officer Candidate School (OCS). This was his first combat operation.

Apamama, November 1943

Apamama is a series of small islets that form a coral atoll. It is located some seventy-six miles south of Tarawa, almost midpoint north and south in the Gilbert chain. The islets ring a relatively large, emerald-colored lagoon lying some twelve miles northwest-southeast and five miles northeast-southwest. It has been described as being in the shape of a "partially deflated football."[10] Robert Louis Stevenson depicted it as an idyllic place. Apamama is higher in elevation (twelve to fourteen feet above the surf line) than either Tarawa or Makin. It is lush, with tall coconut palms, and the blue of the sea contrasting with the brilliant white coral makes a spectacular South Sea island. Before the war its population consisted of about one thousand Gilbertese and, reportedly, eight Caucasians, two Australian nuns, four French or Swiss Catholic priests, and several mixed-race, white "civilians." The name "Apamama" means "land of moonshine." Some confusion regarding the spelling of the name of the atoll is attributable to the change in the Gilbertese alphabet in 1934, when p was changed to b. Thus, the Gilbertese spelling became "Abemama," whereas the Navy continues to use "Apamama."[11]

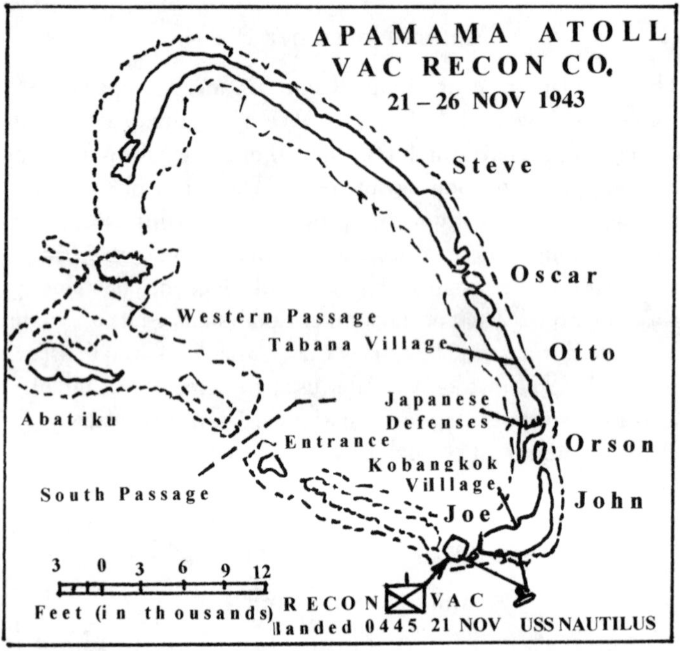
APAMAMA ATOLL
VAC RECON CO.
21 – 26 NOV 1943
Steve
Oscar
Western Passage
Tabana Village
Otto
Japanese
Defenses
Abatiku
Entrance
Orson
Kobangkok
Villlage
South Passage
John
Joe
3 0 3 6 9 12
Feet (in thousands)
RECON
VAC
landed 0445 21 NOV
USS NAUTILUS

Apamama Atoll
Courtesy of the History and Museums Division, HQMC

Capt. Jim Jones's VAC Amphib Recon Company (minus Lieutenant Weeks's 4th Platoon, involved in the Army/Marine landing on Makin discussed above) boarded *Nautilus,* departing Pearl on 8 November 1943 and arriving off Tarawa on 18–19 November. Continuing in a reconnaissance role, *Nautilus* at this time discovered an eleven-degree compass error in the old British charts for the entrance into Tarawa Atoll. Modified charts were quickly produced by the command ship, saving the day for the task force's navigation. The sub's mission completed at Tarawa, it was additionally tasked as plane guard to pick up a downed naval aviator. This mission was canceled and the sub proceeded south to Apamama. The pilot recovery mission cancellation was unfortunately not passed to other ships, and this led to *Nautilus* being taken under fire by friendly forces.

The sub's skipper, Commander Irwin, was running on the surface to ensure clearance of a nearby reef and was trying to clear the passage, or "slot," between Betio and the atoll just to the south. It was 2153 hours, and although there was limited visibility, the sub was picked up as a "pip" on the surface radars of Rear Adm. Hill's Southern Task Force. Concerned that this radar contact might be a Japanese patrol vessel, Hill gave the order to open fire. Both the cruiser *Santa Fe* (CL-60) and the destroyer *Ringold* (DD-500) commenced firing. Although some naval historians (Morison, for example) categorically state that *Nautilus* was struck at the base of its conning tower with a 5-inch shell from the *Ringold,* the marines aboard who examined the shell back at Pearl Harbor (which fortunately did not explode) assured me that this was a 6-inch shell (which thus had to be from the main battery of the *Santa Fe*).[12] This disarmed projectile may be seen today at the submarine officer's club, adjacent to Lockhart Hall at Pearl Harbor's sub base.

The shell severely damaged the main induction valve, which reportedly permitted thirty-seven tons of seawater to enter the submarine. Water hitting the base of the conning tower displaced the gate valve on the voice tube to the bridge, permitting water to come rushing down the tube. This quickly knocked out the submarine's gyro, located just below. Irwin later described this inundation: "We managed to stop the water through the foresight of the machinist mate who was on duty in the conning tower. When he saw that he couldn't close the valve, he rammed his elbow in it. So we made the dive with this machinist mate's elbow in the voice tube. The boy at the dike. That's what kept the water flow down."[13]

One close explosion had ruptured a water line to the port main motor cooling system and started leaks in the bilges. The main induction valve flooded.[14] Irwin immediately crash-dived and took the sub down to three hundred feet. "We used a bucket brigade to carry the water from the motor room to the engine room and the next compartment forward," he recalled. "We wanted to lighten the stern. . . . Our control depth was only 200 feet and we had such an angle on that our stern must have been down close to 300 feet. . . . The *Nautilus* had a riveted hull, and from the time we hit 200 and below, the rivets would squeal as they reset themselves.

There'd be a hell of a whine and then a leak would develop. A rivet would reseat itself under pressure."[15] Only through valiant efforts of the sub's crew were they able to rectify this crippling damage.[16]

To give the reader some insight into what the sixty-eight embarked marines and ten attached Army engineers aboard *Nautilus* experienced during these critical moments, I interviewed Marine Gy. Sgt. Sam Lanford:

> Marines were advised to find a place to sit, get out of the crew's way, and be quiet. I was in the forward torpedo room at the time, sitting on the deck with my back to one of the torpedoes. The compartment hatch had already been secured at the start of the dive . . . We could hear banging and sounds of repair aft. . . . As time went on, we could only sit and think. Time seemed endless. . . . The air began to get stale and the water began to rise on me where I was sitting on the steel deck. I began to measure the water depth as it raised on my leg. . . . At first just an inch or so, then deeper and eventually over my thigh with my leg stretched out. I admit saying a prayer or two. . . . I do not remember having the emotion of fear. . . . I felt totally confident the crew would have everything in order soon and we would be on our way. . . . Suddenly, like a bolt of lightning, the lights came on, shocking us back into reality. The skipper's voice came on the address system. We were going to surface. . . . The boat shuddered a few times. . . . A feeling of motion was again felt, and after a while we could hear the sound of surface water. Finally! The noise of opening the hatch drifted forward to us in the forward torpedo room. Very suddenly the air was filled with a dense fog as the fresh, cool air of the surface hit the stale, moist air of the compartment. Ventilation machinery sucked out the fog and we were free of our captive sea.[17]

Once surfaced, after some three hours on the crash dive, *Nautilus* continued south through the night en route to these marines' first combat recon. Captain Jones later confided to General Smith, "All other things being considered, my marines and I would rather be in a rubber boat (rather than in the submarine when she crash-dived for this period)."[18]

In the late afternoon of 20 November, *Nautilus* arrived off Apamama. It circuited the atoll, noting the entrance to the lagoon, ringed by Entrance Island on the south and Abatiku on the north. Planners for the seizure of Apamama had given code words to each of the six islets, starting with Steve forming the northern and northeastern part of the football, following south with Oscar, Otto, Orson, John, and, finally, Joe, adjacent to Entrance island at the mouth of the lagoon. The plan was for Jones's Amphib Recon Company to land by rubber boat from the submarine onto John at the southern tip of the atoll. Their orders were to land in darkness and scout out the islands, determine the strength of the defending forces, and select beaches for a subsequent occupying American force, which was to follow in a few days. *Nautilus* was tasked to "render direct support within the limits of her capabilities."[19]

As described in the introduction to this book, six of their ten-man rubber boats were inflated, loaded, and wet-deck launched toward their intended landing on John. Only four of the outboard motors would start as they began their trek to the beach. Two outboards later drowned out, and the marines towed and paddled the others. They ran into rain squalls in the darkness, and the heavy westward three-knot current frustrated their landing. Finally, at about 0330 hours, they made the surf zone just off Joe, the last small island at the southern end of the atoll. Coming through the surf, marines were torn up on the coral and landed somewhat exhausted after their ordeal.

The details on the next four days of the Apamama operation, of necessity, rely heavily on Sgt. Frank Tolbert's excellent descriptive story, which appeared in *Leatherneck* magazine some two years later, as well as Shaw's volume 3 and Morison's volume 5. Brig. Gen. Corey had obtained a copy of his own "War Diary," which each of the officers wrote while en route back from the operation. His diary was Annex J to the postoperation report, and although it was classified secret, it was declassified after the war. Personal interviews with some of the participants round out the sources for this account.

On landing, the Marines brought in three supernumeraries: Lt. George Hard, an Australian who had lived in the Gilberts; a Navy CEC engineer officer, Lt. E. F. "Bing" Crosby, a civil engineer who was there to determine location and suitability for an airfield; and Maj. Wilson Hunt of the Marines, a defense battalion specialist who was brought to plan for the occupying force, scheduled to come from Tarawa in a few days.

Each marine brought three K rations, one D ration, and two fragmentation grenades. Ammunition included 45 rounds for each carbine, 48 rounds for each rifle, 260 rounds for each BAR, and 2,000 rounds for each machine gun. Prior to the main landing, while some six hundred yards offshore, two rubber boats, one under 1st Lt. Leo B. Shinn and the other skippered by Lt. Harry C. Minnear, landed through the surf as an advance party and scouted the landing beach.

At 0440, they signaled in the main party, some of whom were cut up on the coral as they made their landing. The exec, 1st Lt. Merwyn H. Silverthorn Jr., established the beachhead and command post (CP), using the ten army engineers who had landed with them. Captain Jones immediately sent out platoon-sized patrols. Lieutenant Corey went north to the lagoon shore with his 3d Platoon. Lieutenant Minnear took his 2d Platoon patrol west toward the western end of Joe. Shinn went north and east with his 1st Platoon toward the channel between Joe and John (their initial intended landing islet). His patrol reported finding a camouflaged seagoing Japanese barge, diesel-powered and fully fueled, moored in the channel. Immediately after finding the barge, Shinn's marines spotted two Gilbertese natives crossing the channel from John. The patrol dove into the bush and waited. As they came abreast, Lieutenant Hard, the Australian interpreter, stood up and spoke to the natives in Gilbertese. They stared at Hard, grinned, and in their best mission-taught Oxford English responded, "Why Mr. Hard. My word! I am glad to see you, but were you wise to come and visit us now? The Sapanese are here!" (Gilbertese pronounce *j*s like *s*s when they speak English).

The two natives informed Hard that the Japanese were entrenched in force around a radio station on Otto, one islet away. They described the Japanese defenses as being reinforced positions using coconut logs and reported that the Japanese weapons included rifles, machine guns, and mortars. The number of Japanese Marines (Rikusentai), twenty-five, were fewer than the number of U.S. Marines, but they were well dug in and "had plenty of ammunition."

Returning to the CP, Shinn's reported on his findings. Jones immediately dispatched Corey's 3d Platoon to "field-strip" (disable) the Japanese barge. (Corey said, "We removed the spark plugs from the engine and made an accelerator adjustment.")[20] It appeared obvious that the barge was going to be the Japanese means of escape to the north. About two hundred yards from the barge, they spotted a Japanese patrol already at the barge. Taking them under fire, Corey's BAR man, Pvt. Homer J. Powers, killed one of the Japanese with an offhand shot. The other two fled into a nearby coconut grove.

Back at the CP, new word came in from the natives: the Japanese had gathered all of their weapons and were moving rapidly to the barge site. Jones and all available marines moved out at "high port" (maximum speed) to the channel where the barge was located. As the Japanese had obviously passed through Kabangak village on John, they must have learned of the Marine presence in force on the atoll. The Japanese immediately turned around and returned to Otto to reoccupy their prepared defensive positions. Jones began a reconnaissance-in-force, moving across Orson, the island just south of Otto, which was occupied by the Japanese defenders.

The Apamamans told Jones of a thin sandspit running northwest from Orson, from which the marines would be able to observe the lagoon (western) flank of the Japanese defenders. Taking the entire company, Jones began crossing the sandspit. Japanese rose from higher terrain to the north of the advancing marines on the sandspit and opened fire on the recon company. One marine killed one of the defenders at one hundred yards. At this point, the recon marines came under fire from their eastern (right) flank from the Japanese coconut log positions on the south end of Otto. Receiving fire from the flank and faced with a rising tide which would cover the sandspit at high tide, Jones withdrew with his company to the northern beach of Orson, where they again reestablished their beachhead. While en route back to their beachhead, Jones paused in Kabangak village and questioned the four Catholic priests and nuns. His marines by this time were exhausted, having gone two days without sleep. All hands rested and took up defensive positions. At about 2030, radio contact was established with *Nautilus*. The sub sent its launch, and by use of a rubber boat, they were able to ferry fifteen days' worth of supplies (food and ammunition) to the beach.

Lights, believed by the marines to be a Japanese submarine trying to contact the Japanese defenders (more probably than not to attempt to evacuate them from Apamama), were seen at about 0300.[21] Jones's rubber boats had been damaged in crossing the coral reef in their initial landing and were in no shape to be used in an attempted envelopment from the sea. The three supernumeraries, Lieutenants Hard and Crosby and Major Hunt, made their own recon to the south end of Orson. There they found that the Japanese had a truck, which would permit them to rapidly reinforce anywhere along Otto's beaches. The marines at this point bought additional supplies from the natives. Gy. Sgt. Charles Patrick took a small patrol up the seaward side of Orson to see if they could flank the Japanese from that side. In the process, one of his marines was taken under fire and wounded. They returned, opining that to cross the channel between Orson and Otto, they would suffer a number of casualties. Clearly additional firepower was needed.

On the morning of the third day, Jones took the entire company and moved forward to the channel between the islands about 150 yards from the Japanese. 1st Lieutenant Silverthorn took Lieutenants Crosby and Hard plus the ten Army engineers and again reestablished a beachhead on the south side of the channel. They emplaced recon's machine guns in the center of their line. At about 0800, the recon marines began to lay down a base of fire on the Japanese positions. They radioed *Nautilus* and requested naval gunfire support from their 6-inch deck gun. Nautilus obliged and, relying on the mattress covers hung in the palm trees, fired some seventy-five rounds with super-quick fuses from some four thousand yards at sea. These rounds would "air-burst" as they hit the palm fronds at the top of the coconut palms. They would be most effective for Japanese in the open but did not do much for the coconut log bunkers. The *Nautilus* gun crew found that one of their 6-inch guns was malfunctioning in the elevating mechanism. It would slip, causing the shell to go "over" and land a great distance from the intended impact. On their own initiative, the crew did a check-fire on that gun.[22] About this time, Corey requested a full check-fire because *Nautilus*'s rounds were falling very close to his lines. The naval gunfire had not appeared to diminish the heavy Japanese fire, so Captain Jones ordered a cease-fire from *Nautilus*. Prior to their debarkation, *Nautilus* and the recon marines had worked out a simple display code in the event of radio communication problems, using variations on the four twelve-by-sixteen-foot naval mattress covers that were to double as signal panels. One configuration would indicate "situation in hand," while others would advise of specific needs, such as "ammo," "water," and so on. Usually front lines were marked by colored air panels, but on Apamama the four mattress covers used as banners later also provided the marines' current lines to the destroyer.

The heavy Japanese machine-gun fire went unabated during most of the third day. As long as the marines remained prone, most of the rounds went over their heads. It was obvious that the recon marines would need mortars to assist their crossing. One of the recon BAR men, PFC William D. Miller, was hit while in an exposed position. Another recon marine and two of the company's corpsmen braved the fire and attempted to rescue him. Unfortunately, Miller was hit again and died before he could be recovered. Two other recon marines, PFC Harry Marek and Cpl. John F. King, were evacuated by rubber boat through the surf to *Nautilus*. Marek, having taken an automatic weapon round through the chest, was in bad shape when brought aboard. He later died and was buried at sea.

Late in the afternoon, a number of American ships appeared on the horizon, so Jones, awaiting arrival of his requested mortars, broke off the firefight and consolidated his positions. He decided to coordinate with the approaching task force. Taking a small launch with Hunt, Crosby, Hard, a Sergeant Benton, and George, a native harbor pilot, he started for the TF. About a mile from the occupation force's ships, they suddenly came about and sailed over the horizon. This left the small launch in open sea some distance from the lagoon entrance. Hunt spotted the telltale feather of a submerged periscope some seven hundred yards from their position and yelled, "Submarine! Probably a Japanese one." George asked Hard in Gilbertese, "What do the Americans discuss?" The Australian's reply: "Yonder is an underwater craft with Japanese!" George responded, "My Word! Under the water. A proper place for the monkey people!" The submarine made no moves toward the small party, so they returned to the atoll. During the late afternoon of that third day, the destroyer *Vandervoort* (DD-608) appeared on the other side of the atoll. It sent a small landing party to offer naval gunfire support. Jones had the DD fire some fifty rounds. *Vandervoort's* fire hit the tops of the coconut palms causing air bursts, which apparently proved quite impressive to the Japanese. The *Vandervoort* agreed to use its naval gunfire the following morning on the Japanese positions.

Early on the morning of the fourth day, natives came to the marines, saying, "The Saps are all dead!" A young Apamaman boy who could speak English told the marines that he observed the Japanese commander giving a pep talk to his troops. He was brandishing his samurai sword and waving a pistol. Urging his troops to "kill all Americans," the officer (apparently) accidentally shot himself in the stomach and died. His troops were disheartened by this turn of events and decided to commit mass hari-kari.

Lieutenant Corey took his 3d Platoon patrol across the channel and confirmed the death of the Japanese defenders. Survivors of the Marine/Navy gunfire had apparently methodically dug their own graves, then lay down in them and shot themselves just below the jaw. It was difficult to understand why, because Corey's marines found that the Japanese had extensive stocks of ammunition. The marines began burying the dead. Soon, out of the coconut palms, came young Apamamans, who began to help the Americans bury the Japanese. The natives, in mission English, sang Christian hymns while they helped. Soon the marines began singing the "Marine Corps Hymn" and other barrack ballads. As the task was finished, the Apamamans returned to their thatch huts (fales), and cooking fires lit the evening as the fourth and last day of the assault of Apamama ended.[23]

Marine recon losses in the Apamama operation were two killed, two wounded, and one injured. The assistant division commander, Brigadier General Hermle of the 2d Marine Division, landed with the 3d Battalion, 6th Marines and assumed occupation duties.[24] As a postscript to this operation, an eight-thousand-foot airstrip was carved out of Apamama's coral by the task force's naval construction battalion (CB). By 15 January 1944, this airstrip was being used by heavy bombers to the Marshall Islands for continuation of the attack.[25] Captain Jones was later awarded the Legion of Merit by Lt. Gen. Holland M. Smith for this consummate amphibious reconnaissance operation.

7

The Marshall Islands

Before seizure of the Gilberts, the Joint Chiefs of Staff ordered Admiral Nimitz, CinCPac in Pearl Harbor to begin to plan for the next westward movement in the South Pacific. Tentative plans were made for the simultaneous seizure, in January 1944, of Kwajalein, Wotje, and Maloelap in the Marshall Islands. After discussions with President Roosevelt and Prime Minister Churchill on 24 August at their conference in Quebec, Canada, the JCS scaled back their prior recommended simultaneous seizure and instead tasked CinCPac to take the Marshalls in two stages: the seizure of Wake, Kusai, and Truk and the eastern Carolines, followed by the seizure of Palau and Yap. This plan was found unacceptable by CinCPac, who recommended bypassing Wake, arguing that the airfields that were to be available after Tarawa was taken could do a better job for eventual capture of Kwajalein. Further, heavy Japanese defense forces were known to be in place on Wake. Kusai was unacceptable because of its extremely wet climate (precluding its use for airfield construction). The JCS finally concurred in the elimination of both Wake and Kusai.

Planning continued during the successful but costly Operation Galvanic in the Gilberts. In December 1943, a modified plan was made to neutralize the peripheral islands in the Marshalls—Jaluit, Wotje, Maloelap, and Mili—and to seize Kwajalein, the main Japanese base in the Marshalls.

Rear Admiral Turner, a sound amphibious tactician blessed with celerity, wrote a strong analysis of the mistakes in the Gilberts titled "Lessons Learned at Tarawa." Chief among the lessons were (1) more and better aerial reconnaissance was needed, (2) more submarine recons (periscope photography), such as was done at Betio, had to be performed (3) more ships (DDs, CAs), landing craft, and LVTs, as well as additional converted LCI gunboats, were needed, and (4) three times the bombardment used at Tarawa, supplemented by increased pre–D-day attacks by carrier, battleships, cruisers, and destroyers, was required.[1]

Admiral Spruance approved Turner's recommendations, and Admiral Nimitz concurred. JCS gave its final approval, slipping D-day to 31 January 1943 to permit assembly of sufficient combat shipping to accommodate two divisions. The operation was given the code name Flintlock, and all participating ships, aircraft, and ground elements increased preparation.

Incorporating the lessons learned from Operation Galvanic, the decision was made to call for the immediate seizure of Kwajalein and bypass its peripheral Japanese air and seaplane bases, Wotje, Maloelap, Mili, and Jaluit. This was a distinct departure from former tactics. In the past, doctrine called for the seizure of the peripheral bases within air-strike distance. Admiral Turner felt with the vastly increased assets of carrier-air and, now that land-based bombers could launch from Tarawa and Apamama, he would be able to neutralize these outlying bases and go for the heart— Kwajalein. The islands of Roi and Namur, connected by a causeway, are at the northern end of the atoll, as is Majuro to the southeast, which intelligence reported as undefended.

As with the periscope recons four months earlier on Tarawa by *Nautilus,* Jaluit was covered by *Spearfish,* Lt. Cdr. J. W. Williams commanding, 18 November and 13 December 1943, on Mili by *Tarpon,* Lt. Cdr. J. B. Oakley Jr. commanding, 13 December 1943 and 4 January 1944, and on Kwajalein itself by *Seal,* Cdr. R. B. Dodge commanding, 17 November 1943. *Seal* "reconnoitered 88 Islands of the 96 comprising Kwajalein Atoll [and] photographed 56 of them."[2] *Seal's* photography of Kwajalein needed to be supplemented, so the *Tarpon* completed the job.[3] This was all part of the still-developing process in the intelligence planning and acquisition for an invasion of a Japanese-occupied territory. Aerial photography, submarine periscope photography, hydrographic recons by Marine and UDT teams, and air strikes and surface strikes on supporting Japanese airfields, ships, and vessels capable of repelling intelligence and (later) assault efforts became part of the panoply of intelligence assets that were worked into the operation plan for the invasion.

Kwajalein Atoll is some 540 miles northwest of Tarawa. The atoll's large triangular lagoon is surrounded by a series of ninety-six reef-encircled islands. Within the atoll, Roi-Namur lay some forty-five miles north of the Kwajalein Island.[4]

Three prongs of attack were planned: (1) a Northern Attack Force, Rear Adm. Richard L. Connely commanding, with the newly formed 4th Marine Division, Maj. Gen. Harry Schmidt commanding, would take Roi-Namur; (2) a Southern Attack Force, Rear Adm. Turner commanding, with the Army 7th Division, Maj. Gen. Charles H. Corlett, USA commanding, would seize Kwajalein Island with its nearly completed Japanese bomber base; and (3) a Reserve Force of the 22d Marines (minus), reinforced by the remainder of the Army's 106th Infantry, would be available where needed, for either operation. This latter force would be the one that took Eniwetok.[5]

A fourth attack group was given Majuro Atoll. Designated the Majuro Attack Group, it was under command of Rear Adm. "Handsome Harry" Hill, who had commanded the attack force at Tarawa (and would be later involved in the seizure of Saipan and Tinian). Capt. Jim Jones's VAC Amphibious Reconnaissance Company would go ashore early for amphibious reconnaissance, followed by the 2d Battalion, 106th Infantry.

The VAC Amphibious Reconnaissance Company, following their successful seizure of Apamama in conjunction with the Tarawa operation in November 1943, had returned to Pearl Harbor after the operation. Adding replacements for the killed and wounded, upgrading weapons, and training were the routine from November to the end of 1943. Lt. Gen. Holland M. Smith, VAC commander, was convinced that "there can not be more than a squad or two on those islands [Majuro Atoll] today. . . . Let's use one battalion for the Majuro job."[6]

Majuro Atoll, January–February 1943

Majuro Atoll, 256 miles southeast of Kwajalein Atoll, consists of fifty-six islets along the 21-mile, 6-to-8-mile-wide lagoon ringed by an enclosing reef on the seaward side of the islets. Majuro Island was long and thin and formed the closure for the lagoon's southern side.

Lt. Harvey Weeks of the VAC Amphib Recon Company landed at 2330 on the night of 30 January on the entrance island to the lagoon. He and his forty-two camouflage-clad, helmeted marines quickly secured Calalin (called Luella during the operation) islet on the northern end of the atoll. Each recon marine carried one-third of a K ration, one-third of a D ration, two grenades, and 45 rounds of carbine ammo or 48 rounds of M-1 ammo or 280 rounds per BAR. Two rubber boats were towed to just off the surf line by a Higgins boat. Despite the fact that several marines went overboard when the towing bridles to the rubber boats parted, Weeks was able to make the beach with all of his troops and their weapons.

Weeks's reinforced recon platoon's landing from the *Kane* (APD-18) was some nine hours prior to the arrival of the main attack force. (Weeks and his forty-two marines were actually, as Tolbert notes, the "first Americans of the Pacific war to invade territory held by the Japanese before Pearl Harbor." This honor, however, was given in error to the Army Scouts of the Seventh Army Division for their landing five hours later on Kwajalein. These Scouts had been trained by VAC amphib recon personnel, so the Marines didn't feel so badly about the loss of this "first." The 7th Scouts were subsequently honored with a Presidential Unit Citation for their "first" landing.)[7]

Weeks sent a detail, under 2d Lt. Boyce L. Lassiter (weapons platoon commander), to take the adjacent entrance islet, Eroj (Lucille). Lassiter found it to be unoccupied as well. He reported these findings to Captain Jones aboard the *Kane*. Jones decided to land the remainder of his VAC Amphib Recon Company by rubber boat on Dalap.

At 0330, using six ten-man LCRs and three seven-man LCRs, the main body waited off the beach while an advance party, commanded by the executive officer, Merwyn H. Silverthorn Jr., now a captain, landed through the surf. They signaled by hooded flashlight (two long dashes separated by two-minute pauses), and the remainder of Jones's company landed through the surf at 0400.

Four of the LCRs capsized in the heavy surf, but all hands made it safely to the beach. The only "casualty" was in the dumping of one of their rubber boats in the surf. A marine photographer, brought to record their findings, lost most of his camera equipment in this mishap. By patrolling, they quickly verified that Dalap was also unoccupied and that the prior report of three to four hundred Japanese on the islet was inaccurate. Jones questioned a Marshallese native who accurately reported that the Japanese main body had earlier evacuated Majuro, leaving only a Japanese Navy warrant officer and a few troops.

As occasionally happens in wartime, communications were lost at about 0530 between Captain Jones and Admiral Hill's Majuro Attack Force. Unable to stop the scheduled 0600 naval gunfire by the cruiser *Portland* and the destroyer *Bullard* on Dalap, the marines and native Marshallese were subjected to eighteen minutes of "friendly-fire" bombardment. Using a TBX radio, they were finally able to restore communication to 2/106 via *Kane* and get a check-fire. Fortunately, none of the marines or natives, or any of the major Japanese buildings, had been hit. Most of the 455 projectiles hit coconut trees and were air bursts. Jones was able to have the similarly scheduled air strike on Majuro canceled before any further possible damage occurred.[8]

During the subsequent patrols, Lt. Leo B. Shinn (a former first sergeant) and his 1st Platoon patrol made contact with a Marshallese trader, Jeff Jefferson. Wearing canvas duck trousers and a derby hat, Jefferson, "a tall imperturbable old fellow of white and Marshallese extraction," proved to be a real character. He invited the marines to have a drink of the local coconut brew ("palm toddy"), and they quickly obliged.[9] Late on the afternoon of 31 January, Weeks and his 4th Platoon were augmented with twenty more marines from Lassiter's weapons platoon and a local Marshallese interpreter. This time, Weeks was tasked to land on the main island. They landed at 0030 on 1 February 1944 from two Higgins boats. During their patrol they learned the location of the Japanese warrant officer who was on another island (code name Laura) some ten miles along the atoll. Using the two Higgins boats, they transited to the distant islet. This time they brought native guides who pointed out the fales where the Japanese lived.

Finding the warrant's quarters unoccupied, Weeks set in his patrols around the quarters. Searching the fale, they found two .50-caliber machine guns with a good stock of ammunition. Here they found some one hundred pounds of dynamite that had been made into crude "grenades." Natives later confirmed that these two machine guns had been salvaged from a B-24 which had ditched in the lagoon a month earlier. The American B-24 crew had been taken prisoner and evacuated to Maloelap Atoll.

At about 0530, Japanese Navy warrant officer Nagata crept back to his quarters. Walking up the path, he was armed with a Samurai sword in one hand and a pistol in the other. Leaping from his hiding place in the brush, Lieutenant Weeks, a former college wrestler, jumped him from the rear, taking him down with a half nelson. Nagata put up no further resistance and was taken out to the APD, under guard, by Plt. Sgt. Frenchy LeClair. Later, three more Japanese were taken prisoner by Lieutenant Corey's 3d Platoon patrol on D+1 (1 February 1944) on the main island of Majuro. Here, in one of the fales, they found additional gear from the crashed B-24: fire-damaged flight suits, flight jackets, a .30-caliber machine gun, and a khaki shirt with master tech sergeant chevrons and the name "Hanson" printed in the collar.[10]

At 0955, on the morning of D-day, 31 January 1944, Rear Admiral Hill was able to report to (now) Vice Admiral Spruance that "Majuro had been secured." An LCVP was sent to pick up Jones and take him aboard the command ship *Cambria*. There he conferred with the officers of 2/106. The Army battalion landed unopposed the next morning. The task force then entered the large lagoon and anchored. Jones and his company reembarked on *Kane*, moving to the east end of the lagoon, where they then secured Dalap and Uliga. The next evening, the battleships *Washington* and *Indiana* came into the lagoon for respite, having had a collision the previous night. By the next day (3 February), there were some thirty ships at anchor in the lagoon.

Upon hearing about the Marshallese trader, Jeffries, Rear Admiral Hill dispatched Captain Jones back to the beach to invite him and his wife to lunch aboard the *Cambria*. Declining to bring one of his "wives," Jeffries came out, barefooted, to the ship, wearing his derby hat and clean white ducks, paddling his own canoe.

He was thus received aboard the flagship with appropriate honors. Jefferson brought gifts for the admiral, including a pen full of live frying chickens and a trussed-up two-hundred-pound boar hog. After a delightful lunch, he thanked the admiral for Captain Jones's stopping of the bombardment and canceling of the air strike. "The dignified old-fellow was the picture of a leader and diplomat," Tolbert noted.[11]

One of the larger buildings on the island was rapidly turned into a hospital and the Navy service squadrons took over the other buildings. In short order, Majuro lagoon was a thriving forward base. An airstrip was quickly built and by 8 February was receiving Navy carrier aircraft for its local defense. Reembarking aboard the *Kane,* Jones and his Amphib Recon Company departed Majuro, bound for fights soon to be had on the small islands of Eniwetok Atoll.[12]

Kwajalein and Roi-Namur, January–February 1943

During the assault of Tarawa, permission was requested to take several small peripheral islands for emplacement of artillery to support the major Marine assault on Betio. The amphibious task force commander, Rear Admiral Turner, denied permission because such an action, he felt, would disclose intentions with respect to the main objective. Recognizing that his Tarawa decision had been wrong, however, Turner now granted permission to make early landings on Eniwetok's Allen, Albert, and Abraham (Ennubirr, Ennumennet, and Ennugarret) for emplacement of the 4th Marine Division's 14th Marines—the division artillery. Before this could happen, the two lagoon entrance "guard islands," Mellu (Ivan) and Ennuebing (Jacob), would have to be taken.[13] Early on the morning of 31 January, naval bombardment and an air strike softened the entrance islands and assaults were made. These eventually opened the entrance to Kwajalein lagoon. Seizure took just over an hour, with few casualties suffered (except for the Japanese). As soon as Ivan and Jacob were secured, LVTs and LCMs carrying the 14th Marines (1/14 and 2/14) entered the lagoon and emplaced 75-mm and 105-mm howitzers on the two entrance islands. Pack howitzers (75-mm) were brought in by LVT (amtracs), while the 105s came in by LCM ("Mike" boats).[14]

Landing about 1530 on Allen, Albert, and Abraham, the three islands were secured by 1638 on D-day. Additional supporting mortars, 37-mm antitank guns, and five 75-mm self-propelled guns were added to the firebase for the next day's assault on Roi and Namur. The next morning, D+1, the assault on both began.[15] Meanwhile, in the southern part of Kwajalein Atoll, Army rubber boat landings of the 7th Scouts were made on the moonless night of 31 January 1944 onto Cea (Carter). Although there was some confusion (initially rubber boats landed on the wrong island), the problem was sorted out, and once the Scouts found the island unoccupied, the Army division artillery, with four battalions of 105 howitzers and one battalion of 155 howitzers, moved onto Enubuj (Carlson).[16]

The close-in islands, in the north (adjacent to Roi and Namur) and south, for the southern landings for the main island of Kwajalein, were taken on D-day, ready for the main assaults of their parent units on their respective objectives on D+1. The rubber boat recons and Scouts had done their job.

As a matter of follow-up, Captain Jones praised the assignment of local native interpreters for his company's use during the Majuro operation. This became the norm in later operations. Jones made strong recommendations that the APDs used to carry the recon marines needed more advanced radar to guide the rubber boats to the beach. This was rectified during the Tinian landings, when radar "targets" were carried by the rubber boats and course changes were radioed to the recon marines by use of SCR 300 radios.

During the hours of darkness of D-day, UDTs reconned just off the assault beaches on all three islands, Kwajalein and Roi-Namur, and found them clear of mines or artificial obstacles that would hamper the scheduled landings.[17] Roi was seized by the end of D+1, and Namur was secured by the afternoon of D+2. To the south, in the army's assault of Kwajalein's main island, they advanced steadily, and by the afternoon of 4 February (D+4), the entire main island of Kwajalein had been taken.

The successes at Kwajalein and Roi-Namur validated Rear Adm. Turner's decision regarding taking peripheral islands early for emplacement of artillery to facilitate the major landings.

Rear Admiral Hill would, shortly, again use this same tactic, once Saipan was taken. Artillery fired across the two-and-a-half-mile channel in the seizure of Tinian (see chap. 8).

Eniwetok, February–March 1944

After the rapid seizure of the eastern Marshalls, Admiral Nimitz wanted to keep the momentum going and seize the western Marshalls. Eniwetok, a large circular atoll some 326 miles west-northwest of Roi in the Kwajalein group, was the logical next objective. It had an excellent anchorage within a large lagoon. The lagoon runs twenty-one miles north-south and seventeen miles east-west. Engebi, the largest northern island of the atoll, was occupied by the Japanese in November 1943; they quickly constructed a four-thousand-foot airstrip. Intelligence estimated enemy strength of the entire atoll was between twenty-nine hundred and four thousand.[18]

Planning for the seizure of Eniwetok started while fighting was still taking place on Kwajalein. On 2 February 1944, Rear Admiral Turner recommended to Rear Admiral Spruance that Catchpole (code name for the Eniwetok operation, changed from the prior code name of Downside, which was used for initial planning) start immediately. The plan was to use the 22d Marines plus the Army's 106th Infantry Regiment (less 2/106) as the landing force. D-day was reset to 17 February 1944. Rear Admiral Hill, commander of the operation, was designated commander, Eniwetok Expeditionary Group.

Hill replicated the task organization that had worked so well in the seizure of Majuro. The 4th Marine Division's ADC, Brig. Gen. Thomas E. Watson commanding, was designated the landing force commander. In addition to the normal tanks, artillery, medical company, shore party, and Joint Army Signal Company (JASCO), of import to our story was inclusion of the VAC Amphib Recon Company under Capt. Jim Jones and Capt. Edward L. Katzenbach Jr.'s 4th Division's Company D, the Scouts Company.[19]

Eniwetok, being made up of some forty islets, with a total area of approximately two and a quarter square miles, had many similar-sounding and difficult-to-pronounce names in Marshallese. Planners chose a series of flower names as the code names, for

ZINNIA
FRAGILE (Engebi)
ARBUTUS
CAMELLIA
CANNA
RUUNITO
LADY SLIPPER (Japtan)
POSY
LILAC
Deep Passage
Passage
HEARTSTRINGS (Parry)
SCALE
STATUTE MILES
5 4 3 2 1 0 5
Wide Passage
PRIVILEGE
(Eniwetok)

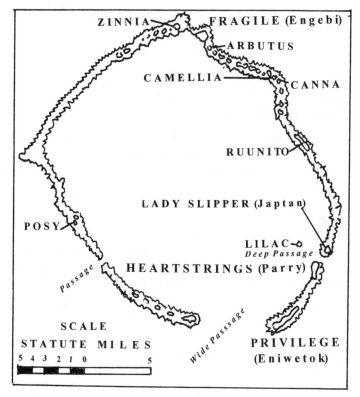

Eniwetok Atoll
Courtesy of History and Museums Division, HQMC

example, Ladyslipper, Heartstrings, Privilege, and Lilac. This was supposed to simplify phonetic spelling in communications and be confusing to the Japanese.

The landing plan called for four phases. First, on D-day, 17 February 1944, three islets in the north were to be seized. Two, Aitsu (Camelia) and Rujioru (Canna), were to be used for artillery bases. Watson ordered Captain Jones's VAC Amphibious Reconnaissance Company to take Canna and Camelia. Capt. Ed Katzenbach's 4th Division Scouts (Company D, 4th Tank Battalion) were ordered to seize Bogen Island (Zinnia), just north of Engebi. Following their seizure, Army and Marine artillery were to land on Canna and Camellia to establish a fire base for next day's landing on the larger island of Engebi (Fragile). Second, Engebi would be stormed from the lagoon side by Col. John T. Walker's 22d Marine Regiment. As soon as it became apparent that the floating reserve for the Engebi operation was not going to be required then, third, they could be shifted to the south for the assaults on the larger islands of Eniwetok (Privilege) and Parry (Heartstrings). The 106th Infantry Regiment was assigned (less one of its battalions as reserve to the north) to conduct this assault on Eniwetok. The original plans called for Parry to be taken some two hours later. Fourth, the remaining islets in the atoll would be secured.

This operation was one of the first times that the VAC Amphibious Reconnaissance Company would not use rubber boats or submarines and instead would use amtracs (LVTs). The task force entered the Eniwetok lagoon at 0900 on D-day, with APD *Kane* in the van. She anchored at 1145 and began preparations for the two simultaneous seizures of the "artillery islands," Camellia and Canna. At 1100, word was received that H hour would be 1230. Although there was an initial misdirection of the recon marines then aboard *Kane* to an incorrect LST-29 (to board their tractors), this was straightened out, and they embarked on their LVTs aboard LST 272.

Splitting the recon company in half, Captain Jones, two officers, and fifty-seven marines aboard three LVTs landed on Aitsu (Camellia) at 1320, quickly overrunning the island and finding it unoccupied by either natives or Japanese. Two LCIs fired in support of their landing. Camellia was reported secured at 1355. The other half of the company, four officers and fifty-seven marines under the exec, First Lieutenant Silverthorn, also used three LVTs and landed on Canna ten minutes later (at 1330). Canna was unoccupied except for twenty-five natives. It was reported "secure" at 1400 hours. Jones, on being informed of the capture of these natives, immediately had them sent to the APD for interrogation by Mr. William "Archie" Mueller, a native Gilbertese interpreter. Five of the natives yielded priceless information on the disposition and strength of the Japanese defense force. The landing force commander, Brigadier General Watson, was informed that there were about one thousand Japanese on each of the three main islands: Engebi in the north, just opposite Camellia and Canna, and Eniwetok and Parry in the south. In addition, one thousand laborers were reported on Engebi.[20]

At about 1500 hours, Marine and Army artillery began landing on both Camellia and Canna. As soon as it was ashore, the recon marines reembarked, leaving their 1st Platoon on Canna, under 1st Lt. Leo B. Shinn, to provide security for the Marine's 2d Separate Pack-Howitzer Battalion. The 104th's Field Artillery Battalion had sufficient numbers that they were able to provide their own security on Camellia.

At 1600 on D-day, the 2d Recon Platoon under Lt. Harry Minnear and the 4th Platoon commanded by 1st Lt. Harvey Weeks, using ship's boats from the *Kane,* patrolled the adjacent island of Buttercup (to the immediate northwest). They found Buttercup unoccupied. At about 1700, other patrols were sent to neighboring Carnation and Columbine, which were also found to be unoccupied. Shinn's 1st Platoon was brought to Columbine to provide security across the small interislet channel for the Marine artillery on Canna. Silverthorn and his fifty-seven marines rejoined the rest of the company. Jones and the entire company then dug in and spent the night on Bitterroot.[21] Both artillery battalions were in firing positions and had completed registration by 1902.[22]

While the VAC Recon Company was seizing the "artillery islands," UDTs, also using amtracs, examined the beaches off Engebi. In doing this recon, the UDT swimmers operated from the LVTs within fifty yards of the landing beaches. The last reconnaissance evolution of D-day was the rubber-boat landing of the 4th Marine Division's Scout Company on Bogen (Zinnia), just west of Engebi. Capt. Edward N. Katzenbach and his Scout Company fought eight-foot waves and twenty-five knot winds to land finally on the island next to Bogen. Years later, Katzenbach confided, "It was one of the harrier landings that I have made. The high surf with the 25-knot wind was terrorizing!" Crossing over, by 0327 on the morning of D+1, Bogen was secured. By the seizing of Zinnia, Camellia, and Canna, the Japanese were precluded from island hopping to the "next island" as they had done before on other atolls (e.g., Majuro and Kwajalein).[23] The 22d Marines landed on Engebi from the lagoon side on D+1 (18 February 1944).

Their assault was preceded by extensive naval gunfire and air strikes. The assault was deadly because of the Japanese defense in the use of coconut log bunkers with connecting tunnels and spider holes (reminiscent of Tarawa). These tunnels were made to radiate outward, starlike, from the main central bunker. They were constructed by first digging trenches in the coral sand and burying fifty-five-gallon oil drums (with both ends removed, much like a culvert), end to end, then covering the whole trench by filling in with sand and covering with driftwood, sand, and plant material. This made these tunnels radiating out from the center "spiderholes" almost impossible to spot. Marines quickly found a way to counter these defenses. They would drop a WP or smoke grenade, and the smoke would waft through the other tunnel shafts and disclose the entire complex.

While the 22d Marines were busy taking the larger island of Engebi, both Jones's and Katzenbach's recon and Scouts were seizing and clearing eight other islets along the atoll. The Amphibious Reconnaissance Company captured one Japanese soldier on one of these forays. On D+1, while occupying Muzingbaarkikku Island (Arbutus) just southeast of Engebi, three recon marines were hit by machine-gun fire from Engebi. One of these marines died while being evacuated to the ship. They finally found this fire to be "overs" coming from marines firing on the holdout Japanese on Skunk Point. By use of 60-mm mortars, the recon unit was able to gain the western edge of Arbutus on the reef passage facing Engebi. They were ordered to hold Arbutus through the night.

For D+2 (19 February 1944), both the recon and Scout companies were ordered by General Watson to continue recon of small islets to the south, moving toward Japtan (Ladyslipper). Landing his entire company on Japtan at about 1800, Jones left the company headquarters, reinforced with the mortar (weapons) platoon to hold the beachhead. He then moved out with his four recon platoons as a line of skirmishers, holding his right flank on the lagoon side, moved south toward the Deep Passage running east-west between Japtan and Parry Islands. Reaching Deep Passage without incident or contact, they circled back north, going up the seaward (eastern side) of the island, again finding no Japanese or natives. Jones reported Ladyslipper secure at 1929 hours. Engebi was finally declared secure at 1640 hours on the afternoon of D+1. The 22d Marines reembarked to come south for the attack on Parry Island.

Seizure of Engebi freed up the artillery to the north. Later that evening, Watson tasked Jones to recon beaches for the landing of Marine artillery on Japtan early the next morning. While Jones's recon company was securing Ladyslipper, the Southern Attack Force with the Army's 106th Infantry was landing on Eniwetok against heavy resistance.

Beaches for the Marine artillery landing on Japtan were selected, and at 0745 hours on the morning of 20 February 1944, Jones radioed Watson, "It is okay to land." The Marines' 75-mm pack-howitzers landed on Japtan at 1000 hours, and Jones's recon company reembarked on APD *Kane* at 1345.[24]

Back aboard *Kane* the morning of D+3 (21 February), the recon marines prepared for the landings on Parry scheduled for the next day. During the day, Weeks's platoon, reinforced with Lassiter's mortars, conducted a recon of Lilac, a small island just west of the Deep Passage on the lagoon side, midway between Japtan and Parry Islands. Lilac was found secure, although it showed signs of recent Japanese occupation. Weeks's patrol did find a sunken Japanese landing barge offshore.[25] While the recon company was on the Lilac operation, the 22d Marines had come south and began participation in the Army attack on Eniwetok. Captain Katzenbach's Scout Company, in the meantime, was continuing to clear the islands and coral outcroppings on the western side of the atoll. On the larger islet of Rigii (Posy), twenty miles west of Deep Passage, the Scouts killed nine Japanese.[26] General Watson, well aware of the continuous hard fighting and casualties in the seizure of Engebi, wisely decided to wait to start the assault on the main Japanese bastion on Parry. Captured documents taken on Engebi confirmed that Parry was strongly held. To augment the 22d Marines, Watson attached the 2d Separate Tank Company, VAC Amphib Recon Company, and the 4th Marines Scout Company. The 3/106 was designated as reserve.

On the morning of D+4, 22 February 1944, the landings began, preceded by intense naval gunfire, air strikes, and artillery barrages from Eniwetok and Japtan (the artillery island) to the north. Parry took the greatest weight of naval gunfire in the

Eniwetok campaign. The totality of prelanding fires bathed the beaches in smoke. This caused confusion, and three LCIs were hit by our own fire from U.S. destroyers firing by radar because of the intense smoke. Marines hit the beach at 0908 hours, two battalions abreast (1/22 and 2/22). The 3d Battalion, 22d Marines was called in early to follow in trace. It landed at 1000 hours and was immediately engaged by Japanese small-arms fire and mortars. The tanks landed with the troops and were successful in all sectors where they were used.

Reconnaissance was put "into the line" to augment the infantry units then involved. At 1230 hours, both the VAC Amphib Recon Company to augment 2/22 and the 4th Division Scout Company to augment 1/2 were ordered ashore.[27] Landing at 1320 in a covered landing, Captain Jones reported his company to Col. John T. Walker, CO, 22d Marines. He was immediately ordered to in turn report to battalion landing team (BLT) 2/22.

Lt. Col. Donn C. Hart, CO of BLT 2/22, quickly sketched the situation for Jones, and they jointly made the decision to split the recon company in two. The exec, Silverthorn, was sent with the 3d and 4th Platoons (Lieutenants Corey and Weeks) to Fox Company. Jones took the 1st Platoon (Lieutenant Shinn) and the 2d Platoon (Lieutenant Minnear) and reported to the skipper of Easy Company. Headquarters personnel and the mortar platoon were divided equally between the two groups.

At the request of the company commander of E Company, Jones put his 1st Platoon on the left flank and Minnear's platoon behind the right flank. Joining the assault as E Companies units were then moving forward the final 250 yards to the ocean, they were supported by four light tanks. The recon company personnel were "mopping up" bypassed enemy snipers. The two tanks on the left withdrew, however, the two right tanks continued through to the beach. About fifty yards from the beach, the recon platoons passed through the E Company assault elements and pushed through to the beach. Conferring with the E Company commander, the recon elements took over the beach defense.

Silverthorn's detachment of 3d and 4th Platoons had more difficulty. Fox Company was between Easy and George Companies. Fox had secured all but the last twenty-five yards to the beach, an area honeycombed with dugouts filled with snipers in connecting emplacements on the beach. Silverthorn and his platoons could see they needed the help of flame throwers and demolitions. After a brief withdrawal to thirty yards from the beach, they reorganized, now with the additional firepower. In short order they overran the Japanese defenses, sustaining four casualties in the action. On order, the recon troops withdrew and were phased into the Fox Company main line of resistance (MLR) for the night. During the night, they were hit by Japanese attacks, resulting in fifteen Japanese dead and no loss to themselves. The next morning, 14 February, D+6, they received orders to withdraw. The Amphib Recon Company was then transferred from the *Kane* and assigned to the *Neville* (AP-16) for return to Pearl Harbor.[28]

Recon purists will abhor the use of skilled recon personnel (including the 4th Marine Division's Scouts and Snipers under Captain Katzenbach) in such a pure infantry role. I again respectfully defer to the judgment of the proven combat leaders on the scene. They obviously felt that this was the best use of these reconnaissance assets, and it is difficult to second-guess their judgment. They were successful. They suffered minimal casualties. One must look at their entire employment, in the Kwajalein and Roi-Namur landings as well as in the seizure of Eniwetok Atoll.

For actions on Eniwetok, Lieutenant General Smith pinned the Bronze Star on First Lieutenant Weeks, and Admiral Nimitz presented Capt. Jim Jones with his second Legion of Merit.

If anything, this action dispels the allegations of amphib recon "elitism," of recon marines being "special" troops not equal to more standard assault tasks. They conducted recon landings on some fifty-plus islets, considering the activities of both the VAC Amphibious Reconnaissance Company and the 4th Marine Division's Scouts and Snipers. By any standards, both units deserved a "Well done" from their infantry peers, and they were appropriately recognized and decorated.

8

The Marianas

After returning from their successful operations in the Marshalls at Roi-Namur and Kwajalein on 7 March 1944, the VAC Amphibious Reconnaissance Company was infused with replacements for their killed and wounded. Intensified training of the replacements began.

Restructuring of FMF Reconnaissance Assets

The VAC staff was well aware of the limitations of the single amphib recon company for corps-level reconnaissance missions. Lt. Gen. Holland Smith had recommended to CMC Lt. Gen. Alexander Vandegrift expanding the recon company to a battalion, allowing additional flexibility and continuity for assignment of missions. Now, with two amphibious corps (III AC and VAC), each could be assigned an amphibious reconnaissance company for their pending missions.

Less than a week after its return from Kwajalein, the company was doubled and reorganized into two recon companies (A and B), each with a twenty-marine weapons platoon (mortars and machine guns) and a headquarters company. Communications were beefed up with the addition of more communicators and radios to a total of ten. The addition of the battalion's own supply personnel obviated the prior necessity of "scrounging gear" to get ready for the next operation.

The table of organization for the new battalion, 23 officers and 291 enlisted (including 13 corpsmen), was approved on 28 April 1944. Capt. Jim Jones shortly was promoted to major as the CO of the new battalion. Capt. Merwyn Silverthorn Jr. continued initially as the battalion executive officer and was later replaced by the more senior Capt. Earl Marquardt. Silverthorn then took command of A Company, 1st Lt. Russell Corey took command of B Company, and 1st Lt. Leo Shinn moved up to the battalion's small headquarters. To fill some of the vacant officer slots, in June 1944, two staff NCOs who were acting as platoon commanders were promoted to second lieutenant.[1]

Indicative of the increased awareness on the part of senior marine commanders on the necessity for dedicated recon assets, the following month, the Marine division Scout companies were redesignated division reconnaissance companies and brought into the division's headquarters battalion. This eliminated the prior intermediate staff when they were in the division's tank battalion. This brought them more directly under the CG and his G-2 (Intelligence) and the G-3 (Operations) staffs. Each division recon company had 5 officers and 122 enlisted, organized into three platoons (contemplating the potential usage of one platoon with each of the division's regiments).[2]

The Marianas

With guidance from the Joint Chiefs of Staff, the Marianas replaced Truk as the next series of islands for seizure. The four largest islands—Guam, Rota, Saipan, and Tinian—became the logical strategic targets. The northernmost two, Saipan and Tinian, were to become the landing objectives of General Smith's VAC, consisting of the 2d and 4th Marine Divisions. The Army's 27th Division was to be Corps's reserve. Seizure of Guam in the southern Marianas was tasked to Maj. Gen. Roy S. Geiger, whose III Amphibious Corps was composed of the 3d Marine Division, the 1st Provisional Marine Brigade, and the Army's 77th Division.[3]

Saipan, in the center of the Marianas, was only 1,250 miles from Tokyo. It was the Japanese equivalent of Pearl Harbor in the sense that it was the administrative headquarters for all of the Japanese forces in the western Pacific. Through Saipan funneled all of the supplies and troops that comprised Japan's Pacific defenses. It formed a part of Japan's inner defense line. Once it was taken, it would "destroy the main bastions and open the way to the home islands."[4] After the war, General Smith emphatically stated, "I have always considered Saipan the decisive battle of the Pacific offensive. . . . It varied the Pacific drama in all its subsequent scenes."[5]

Saipan

D-day was set for 15 June 1944. The newly designated VAC Amphib Recon Battalion departed Pearl on 28 May aboard the APD *Stringham* and the APA *Cambria*. Company A was tasked for a D-1 night landing to seize 1,554-foot Mount Tapotchau, which was at almost the center of the island. Fortunately for Company A, on D-3 this mission was canceled. Following the landing, it took some thirty-nine days of intensive close combat, supported by a plethora of naval gunfire, artillery, and air strikes, for much larger and more appropriately equipped battalions to finally declare Saipan secure.

Pre–D-day reconnaissance was limited on Saipan because the joint amphibious force commander, Vice Admiral Turner, was cautious about disclosing Saipan as the initial main target. Turner also turned down any pre–D-day amphibious reconnaissance at Tarawa (which, in hindsight, some military historians feel contributed to the extremely high casualties on Tarawa's landing beaches). With the exception of UDTs 5, 6 and 7's daylight recon of the approaches, and their search for obstacles off the beaches, performed under strong naval gunfire protection, I could find no indication of any other pre–D-day beach recon of Saipan.[6] Other factors contributing to less intelligence regarding Saipan (in comparison to Kwajalein) was its location more than one thousand miles from the nearest U.S. bases. The cloud cover over the Marianas at that time of year also reduced the effectiveness of aerial photography.

On D-day, the assault waves were subjected to intense frontal mortar and small-arms fire as well as deadly enfilade from 120-mm guns flanking the landing beaches. Enemy strength on Saipan had been estimated at only 9,000–11,000 combat troops with 1,200 Japanese and Korean construction personnel. In actuality, Japanese documents captured during the operation put the total number of Japanese military on Saipan at 31,629, a figure that included some 6,690 naval personnel.[7]

Prior to D-1 (14 June), UDT recons of Red, Green, Yellow, and Blue Beaches, and the alternate landing site of Scarlet Beach,

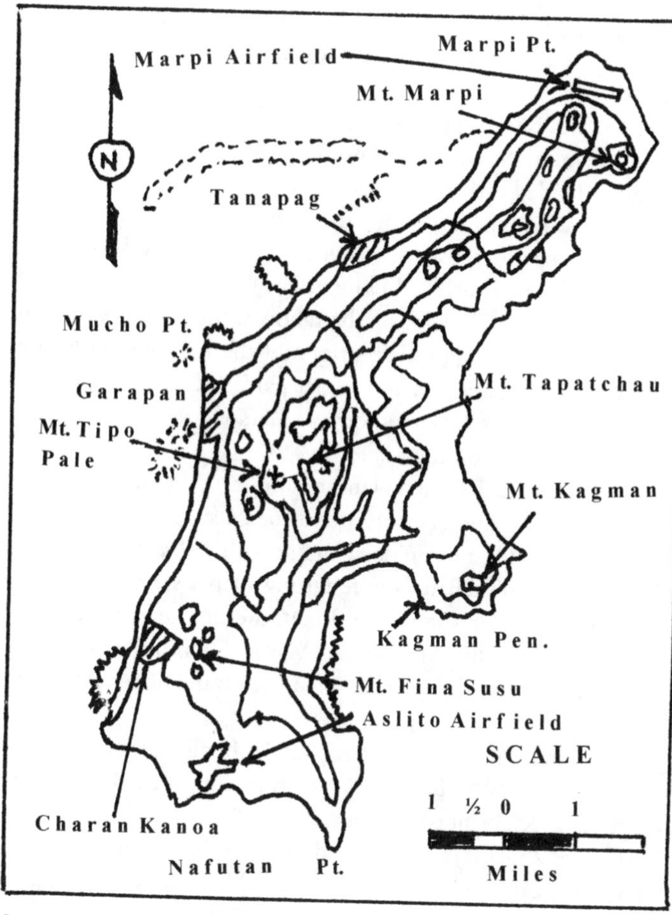
Marpi Airfield
Marpi Pt.
Mt. Marpi
N
Tanapag
Mucho Pt.
Garapan
Mt. Tipo Pale
Mt. Tapatchau
Mt. Kagman
Kagman Pen.
Mt. Fina Susu
Aslito Airfield
SCALE
1 ½ 0 1
Miles
Charan Kanoa
Nafutan Pt.

Saipan
Courtesy of History and Museums Division, HQMC

Lt. Cdr. Draper Kaufman, skipper of UDT 5, had predicted 50 percent casualties in his UDT teams. In actuality, they suffered 13 percent casualties (two killed in action and seven wounded in action).[8]

Kaufman's teams planted their usual markers to show LVT drivers, landing craft drivers, and coxswains routes through obstacles. During the night of D-1 through the early morning hours of D-day, Japanese swimmers had placed small red marker flags among the UDT markers. It was later determined that these were placed as target-distance markers for Japanese artillery and their enfilading beach-defense guns.[9]

Diaries of and personal interviews with the VAC amphib recon personnel reveal that Company B, VAC Amphib Recon Battalion landed early in the afternoon on D-day. On 17 June, B Company joined the rest of the battalion at Charan Kanoa, one of the first towns seized by the assault troops, just inland from Blue Beach 1 and Blue Beach 2.[10] This became General Smith's CP, and for the next several weeks, the battalion carried out a variety of assignments, including CP security and the mopping-up of by-passed Japanese defenders and sniper patrols. Later, B Company would patrol out of the larger town of Garapan as the assault divisions moved north on the island.[11]

Histories of the Saipan landings indicate that recon companies from the Marine divisions performed a series of special missions that included a recon detachment with 1/9 seizing the summit of Mount Tapotchau, later repulsing a Japanese counterattack on that highest point of Saipan. In another instance, a recon detachment with the 6th Marines (2d Marine Division) was ordered to attack a ravine with Japanese defenders on the slopes of Mount Tapotchau.[12]

Admiral Turner and General Smith finally declared Saipan secure on 9 July 1944. Saipan was costly to both sides. The Americans suffered 3,225 killed in action and 13,061 wounded in action. There were 23,811 Japanese dead. The POWs numbered 928, and 838 Koreans and 10,258 Japanese civilians were interned.[13]

Tinian

The amphibious reconnaissance carried out by both A and B Company swimmers on Tinian was, by all standards, the finest example of a clandestine recon of enemy beaches. The recons were executed brilliantly, without loss of any security that would have endangered the assault forces, and they resulted in minimal casualties for the later assault landings of the 2d and 4th Marine Divisions. In retrospect, there was no single amphib recon operation during World War II which contributed more to the Pacific campaign than the ones at Tinian.

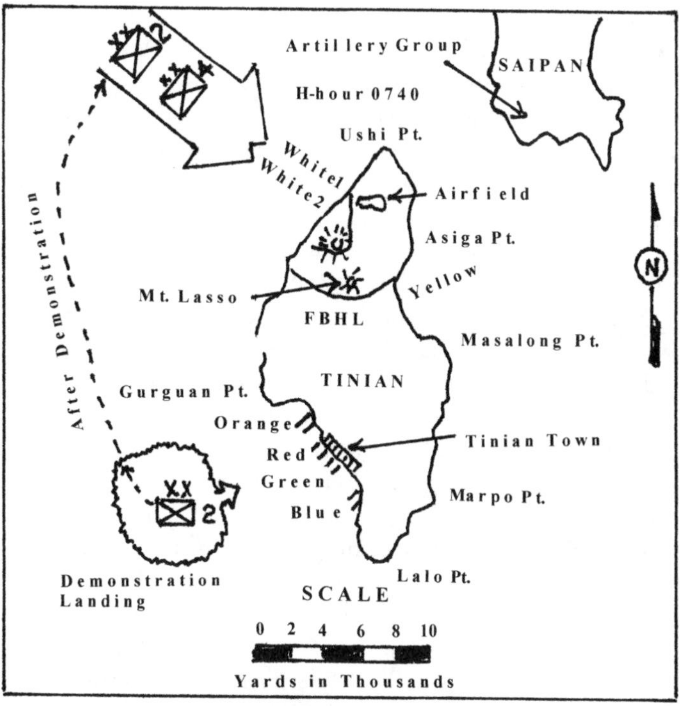
Artillery Group
H-hour 0740
SAIPAN
Ushi Pt.
White1
White2
Airfield
Asiga Pt.
Yellow
Mt. Lasso
FBHL
Masalong Pt.
TINIAN
Gurguan Pt.
Orange
Red
Green
Blue
Tinian Town
Marpo Pt.
After Demonstration
Demonstration Landing
Lalo Pt.
SCALE
0 2 4 6 8 10
Yards in Thousands
N

Plans for the Tinian landing
Courtesy of History and Museums Division, HQMC

Two and a half miles across Saipan channel to the south of the island of Saipan lay the island of Tinian. Approximately ten and a half miles from north to south, it had the best airfields in the Marianas. (These airfields figured prominently in the later prosecution of the war, and one was the launch site for the B-29 *Enola Gay,* which dropped the atom bombs on Hiroshima and Nagasaki, thus ending the war.)

Tinian was a complex plateau of relatively flat country, mostly covered with sugarcane. Major features included Mount Lasso (a 500-foot volcanic peak in the north and an unnamed 580-foot peak to the south). The entire island was surrounded by cliffs, varying from 150 feet above the surf in the south, to 25 feet on the east, and 4 to 6 feet on the north. The cliffs were rust-colored volcanic lava and water-carved coral. Tinian Town was the major town on the island and the center of mass of Japanese colonel Kiochi Ogata's nine-thousand-man defense force. Aerial photography and reconnaissance flown from Saipan by virtually all of the marine assault commanders confirmed that it was the most heavily defended of all possible usable beaches. This two-thousand-yard-wide sandy beach was located on Sunharon Bay on the southwest side of Tinian.

On the eastern side of Tinian, at Asuga Bay, were the next-best beaches for an amphibious landing. Use of the Asuga Bay beaches, however, would entail working around the twenty-five-foot cliffs for beach exits. These beaches, designated as Yellow 1 and 2, were also backed by formidable Japanese defenses.

The only potential beaches capable of permitting LVTs, DUKWs, artillery, trucks, and supply vehicles to negotiate the three-to five-foot cliffs backing them were two very small beaches called Hagoi. They had been designated White 1 and White 2 and had only minimal defense forces backing them (approximately one company). The beaches were covered with white sand and were known to be used as swimming beaches by the Japanese in their off hours.

Admiral Turner and General Smith had to make a decision: Which beach should they select? Turner had summarily dismissed the possibility of using the small Hagoi beaches. White 1 was only 60 yards wide, and White 2 was only 135 to 160 yards wide. Turner held strongly that use of White 1 and 2 "was impracticable."[14]

In addition to beach size, another factor to consider was the short over-water distance from Saipan (two and a half to three miles across Saipan Channel). By landing on the northern end of Tinian, most of the northern half of Tinian would be within the artillery fan and range of General Smith's thirteen artillery battalions, sited hub-to-hub on the southern slopes of Saipan. The short over-water distance meant that the landing force could preload on Saipan without having to organize itself for a typical ship-to-shore landing.[15]

Before turning over command of V Amphibious Corps to Maj. Gen. Harry Schmidt and assuming command of the newly designated Fleet Marine Force Pacific (FMFPac), General Smith recommended to Turner his choice of White 1 and 2. This caused unprintable rejection by Turner aboard his command ship, AGC

Rocky Mount.[16] Smith then turned to his reliable V Amphib Recon Company (now a battalion) under Capt. James Jones (Jones made major shortly after this operation) for the answer to the question, Which beach? A copy of the actual top secret Op Order 27-44, again augmented with personal interviews with the surviving participants, helped reconstruct this classic recon. The op order breaks down the mission for the respective ships and recon companies and UDT, and it provides precise times and locations as well as radio frequencies.[17]

Alerted on 3 July of the impending Tinian mission, the battalion was finally given the op order on 9 July. It tasked Jones's battalion to conduct rehearsals that night (9–10 July) on two Purple beaches on Magicene Bay on Saipan. Working with APDs *Stringham* and *Gilmer,* they embarked at Stone Pier on Blue Beach and transited to their rehearsal area. Jones and his battalion, less B Company, were on *Stringham.* Capt. Merwyn H. Silverthorn Jr. had A Company, and 1st Lt. Leo B. Shinn had his B Company aboard *Gilmer.* UDT Team 7 under Lt. Richard F. Burke, USNR, was aboard *Stringham* with Jones and Silverthorn's A Company. Lieutenant Commander Kaufman's UDT 5 was to work with Shinn's B Company from *Gilmer.*

Rehearsals went reasonably well, and the launching drill bugs were worked out with respective ship's company. For the actual operation to be conducted the night of 10–11 July, Silverthorn and Burke were to recon Yellow Beach 1 on the eastern side of Tinian, and Shinn and Kaufman were assigned White 1 and White 2 on the northwestern side. The recon marines were to debark from the APDs at 2100 hours (*Stringham*) and 2130 hours (*Gilmer*), using eight rubber boats for each beach for the recon personnel and two rubber boats for the UDT teams. They were to be armed only with Ka-Bars (or Fairbairn-Sykes fighting knives). Captain Jones felt that they should take some .38-caliber pistols with them for close-in defense if spotted. They requested permission to take the .38s, but Brig. Gen. Graves B. Erskine, the VAC chief of staff, declined permission, so they landed with just the Ka-Bars or Fairbairns.

The op order was specific on what they wanted the Marines (and where appropriate, the UDTs) to do. In addition to the depth of water and characteristics of the off-lying reef, they were asked for location and nature of the obstacles on the beach and the height and characteristics of the cliffs and the vegetation behind the beach. They were asked for an appraisal of the types of craft that could be landed on each beach and the types of vehicles which could cross the reef and move inland. Finally, General Smith asked for their estimate as to whether infantry could climb the cliffs without ladders or cargo nets. In order to avoid detection, it was mandated that before any marine went onto the beach proper, the patrol had to carefully observe the beaches and be "satisfied there are no hostile patrols" there.[18]

Faces blackened with black and silver nonreflective face paint (from Elizabeth Arden), they were wearing cammies or cut-off shorts made from utility trousers. Headgear was soft covers. They did bring their steel helmets ("pots") with them on the second night, but that was to help provide a radar target for *Stringham's* radar. They did not take the pots with them on the swimming/beach recon mission. On their feet they wore coral or tennis shoes or an occasional pair of boondockers (to avoid cuts by coral). All hands had small inflation bladders (usually not inflated) to provide positive buoyancy when needed.

Fortunately, the night was dark and overcast (moonrise was not supposed to be until 2230 hours) as the marines were towed by Higgins boats to some four to five hundred yards off their respective beaches. Two marines were left in each boat to paddle them to keep station off the beaches where the swimmers went in. The UDT officers and team swimmers swam into the beaches with the marines and remained in the water to carry out the hydrographic surveys.

Silverthorn's A Company swimmers, accompanied by Burke's UDT 7, were towed to their position off Asuga Beach's Yellow 1, slipped over the side, and went to the beach. The UDT found anchored mines, numerous potholes, and coral heads, hydrographically putting a negative on use of Yellow 1. When the moon did come out, its feared illumination was diminished by fairly heavy clouds until nearly midnight. Silverthorn's beach recon found double-apron barbed wire along the beaches.

A Company's 2d Lt. Donald Neff worked his way about thirty yards inland, silently evading a Japanese sentry having a smoke. As he was looking for beach exits for tracked and wheeled vehicles, he was startled by explosives being used by the Japanese just inland from the beach. He thought that they might have been spotted, but they later surmised that these explosions were due to the hasty construction of trenches and blockhouses for beach defenses.

Sentries were patrolling the top of the twenty-five-foot cliffs flanking Yellow 1 and, occasionally, would shine a searchlight down on the beach and look over the side, but none of Silverthorn's team were spotted. They returned to the *Stringham* about 0200 hours with a collective (UDT gave strong concurrence) "negative" recommendation for any further consideration of Yellow 1.[19]

To the northwest, Lieutenant Shinn's B Company had immediate problems with a strong northerly tidal set. He had split his team in two, one for White 1 (the northern of the two) and one for White 2 (the southern). Because of this strong set to the north, White 1's team was carried north of Tinian about eight hundred yards and landed on a coral outcropping. Had they not found this, the team would have been carried north into Saipan Channel. The other team, scheduled for recon of White 2, was able to make it ashore on White 1 instead. They made a hasty recon and returned to the *Gilmer* with a partial report on just White 1. The recovery back aboard *Gilmer* by B Company swimmers did not go without difficulty. The night's low scudding clouds across the dark sky made it difficult to see the recovery LCRs waiting off the beaches. The heavy northerly current and tide had moved them to the north of their assigned pickup points. Both UDT and marine recon had cases of swimmers missing their pickup. Gy. Sgt. Sam Lanford and PFC John Sebern from B Company were keenly aware that they could not stay near the White beaches; it would jeopardize the security of the entire operation if they were caught. Using their partially inflated flotation bladders, stuffed in their dungaree jackets, Lanford and Seborn swam out into Tinian Channel (between Saipan and Tinian) and tread water for nearly two and a half hours. Finally, at dawn, they were spotted and recovered by the APD *Dickerson,* one of the picket boats patrolling the channel. UDT's Lieutenant Commander Kaufman underwent a similar swim for recovery in Tinian Channel and was also recovered by the *Dickerson.*[20]

Capt. Jim Jones was not satisfied with the first night's recons. With Captain Silverthorn's successful and complete recon of Yellow Beach 1, Jones assigned "Silver" (Silverthorn's call sign) to redo both White 1 and 2. Knowing the criticality of the information that he was tasked to obtain, Silver put together six two-man swimmer teams of one officer and one senior staff NCO each. There were no junior-ranked enlisted on the second night (11–12 July 1944). A Company's exec, Lieutenant Weeks, took M.Gy. Sgt. Pat Patrick, the only B Company swimmer to go the second night. Silverthorn took his company first sergeant, Ken Arzt. Lts. Wayne Pepper, Paul Taylor, Ted Toole, and "Mac" McGregor each swam with their respective platoon sergeants. Three teams went in on White 1 and three on White 2.

Thus Silver, in addition to getting his most senior swimmers, also took the additional step of requesting more definitive radar tracking of his boats from the APD to their beaches. This time they towed a "target" LCR with a small metal tripod with wire mesh to provide a good, solid radar target. In addition to the target, they brought their highly radar-visible steel helmets, leaving them in the LCRs as they went over the side. Using *Stringham*'s more advanced radar, with course directions over the SCR 300 radio, they went directly to their assigned beaches.[21] This second night's "combined" teams were eminently successful and confirmed the usability of White 1 and White 2 for the major assaults to follow.

Their observations of the three- to five-foot cliff just inland from the beach gave the LVT units enough information for the immediate and ingenious design of a dropable, portable ramp of timbers and a frame that permitted direct exit over this potential obstacle. It worked perfectly. As they were dropped in, ramping access over the cliff was immediately in place. Wheeled and tracked vehicles were then able to land and go immediately up the ramp and out of the "funnel" of the narrow beaches and spread out inland very quickly.

In my interview of Captain (later Colonel) Silverthorn, he was able to add some insight into the contentious conflict between General Smith and Admiral Turner over the choice of beaches. Rear Admiral "Handsome Harry" Hill felt as Schmidt and Smith did, that the advantages of landing away from the main enemy defenses, on an essentially undefended beach, far out-weighed landing on Tinian Town's "better" beaches, as Turner pro-posed. As Silverthorn briefed Admiral Hill, Hill kept pressing for Silverthorn's opinion on the White beaches. In exasperation, Silverthorn emphatically said, "Admiral, the beaches are narrow . . . [but] there are no mines, no coral heads, no boulders, no wire, no boat obstacles and no offshore reefs. The beaches are as flat as a billiard table!" That sold Hill. He acknowledged, "You have con-vinced me!"[22] Armed with the direct reports from recon, Hill went over Turner's head, going directly to Admiral Spruance and vocif-erously arguing along with Smith and Schmidt for use of the White beaches. Spruance, not wanting to overtly override his subordi-nate, Turner, was finally able to diplomatically assuage the tem-pers and differing opinions so strongly argued, and the White beaches were ultimately chosen.

Two weeks later, at dawn on 24 July 1944, the 4th Marine Division, using preloaded LVTs, cargo-netted loads in trucks and DUKWs, and outstanding "beach mastering" by naval and Shore Party teams, landed over these two very small beaches. They attacked fifteen hundred yards inland before suffering their first casualty.

Colonel Ogata's Japanese defenders were swayed by the ag-gressive "demonstration" landing done by the 2d Marine Division's assault forces just off Tinian Town's western beaches. The 2d Division's transport group debouched their marines, twice climb-ing down the cargo nets on the ship's side. They then rendez-voused off the line of departure. They started toward the beach in the same manner as if they were engaged in a full assault landing. The illusion that the main landing was to be at Tinian Town beaches was augmented further by the UDTs blowing charges in the waters just off Tinian Town. As a result, when the assault waves "turned away," Ogata felt his fire had temporarily beaten off the landings on Tinian Town's beaches. As a consequence, Ogata kept his reserves in the southern end of Tinian, while, on the northwest tip, over the recon-recommended White beaches, the entire 4th Marine Divi-sion was ashore with minimal casualties by midafternoon. The next day, the 2d Division, following their "demonstration" land-ings of the day before, came ashore over the same White beaches to join in the seizure of the rest of the island. The entire Tinian operation took nine days, and the island was declared secure at the same time as the Guam landings, 1 August 1944.[23]

Guam

The U. S. involvement with Guam began in 1899, when it became a U. S. possession. This resulted in the defeat of the Spanish in the Philippines in the Spanish-American War of 1898. Guam was then ceded to the United States by the Spanish. President McKinley felt that it would be an advantageous coaling station in support of our trade with the Orient. A small naval garrison (with a marine barracks) was established on the Orote Peninsula on the western shore. The peninsula forms the southern arc of Apra Harbor.

With a naval officer as governor, Guam sat for more than forty years in the backwater of U.S. bases in the Pacific. It was seized by the Japanese three days after the attack on Pearl Harbor. The military governor, with virtually no adequate defenses, surrendered Guam without a fight. The Japanese built new airfields, and the island became a strategic part of Japan's Co-Prosperity Sphere.

Guam is thirty miles long and varies in width from four to eight miles. It is heavily canopied with thick jungle and ground cover. Graced with a spinous ridge running north to south down the center of the island, the peaks in this ridge exceed one thousand feet, and the ridge itself is cut by a series of cross-valleys. These make a series of abrupt terrain cross-compartments. Such terrain favored the Japanese defenders in any efforts to retake this, our first U.S. possession to be captured by the enemy.

Taking into account the difficulties and strong resistance encountered in the capture of Saipan, a reappraisal was made on the previously determined size of force necessary to retake Guam. Early on, the III Amphibious Corps and the 1st Marine Provisional Brigade had been considered sufficient to retake Guam. The Saipan experience dictated upping the force size to three divisions. Thus the Army's 77th Division in Hawaii, the out-of-theater reserve, was immediately briefed, embarked, and sent to join the prospective landing forces by W+1.[24] (Note: In operations that involved multiple landings on different objectives, for planning purposes, different prefixes for the usual "D-day" would be used in order to keep the plans separate. Thus, on Tinian it became "J day," and on Guam it became "W day.")

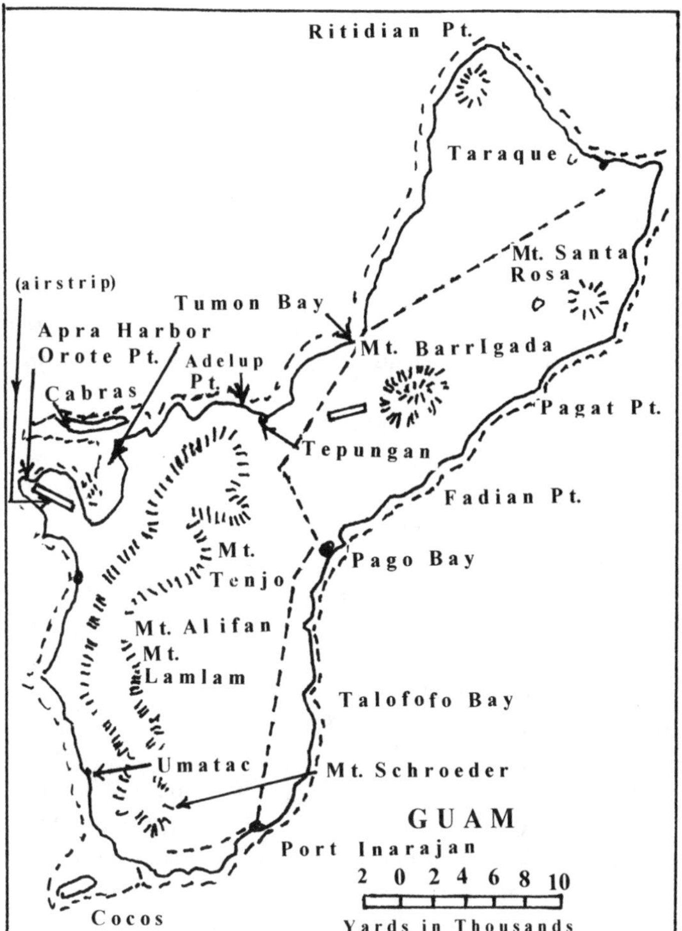
Ritidian Pt.
Taraque
Mt. Santa Rosa
(airstrip)
Tumon Bay
Apra Harbor
Orote Pt.
Adelup Pt.
Mt. Barrigada
Cabras
Pagat Pt.
Tepungan
Fadian Pt.
Mt. Tenjo
Pago Bay
Mt. Alifan
Mt. Lamlam
Talofofo Bay
Umatac
Mt. Schroeder
GUAM
Port Inarajan
2 0 2 4 6 8 10
Cocos
Yards in Thousands

Guam
Courtesy of History and Museums Division, HQMC

When planning began, a number of months before the landings on Guam, 18 June 1944 had been selected as W day for Phase II of Operation Forager (capture of Saipan and Tinian were Phase I). This date was slipped because of two incidents: first, the Battle of the Philippine Sea, which drew down the fleet assets during the Saipan operations and, second, the ferocious intensity of the defense of Saipan. This, as well as waiting for the arrival of the 77th

Division from Hawaii, forced setting the new W day as 21 July. Initially, Guam was to have the 27th Army Division as floating reserve. Tactical dictates required the 27th being used more fully than anticipated at Saipan. This forced the alert and immediate movement of the 77th Army Division from Oahu.

One would have thought that the United States had ample basic intelligence on Guam after our forty-one-year possession of the island. But such was not the case. According to the Marine Corps Command and Staff School records, only one marine reconnaissance officer, in 1936, did anything approaching a staff study on Guam and the requirements for its assault.[25] There were major gaps in aerial pre–W-day photography of Guam because of the very dense jungle growth on much of its terrain. The submarine *Grayling* (SS-209), however, was able to obtain good periscope beach-level photography between 2 and 29 April 1944, first of Saipan and Tinian then later in April on Guam.[26]

As a result of the commitment of the entire VAC Amphib Recon Battalion in the Saipan-Tinian campaigns, no VAC recon assets were used in the retaking of Guam. What limited pre–W-day recon was done was carried out by UDTs. Teams 3, 4, and 6, operating from APDs *Dickerson* (APD-21, UDT-3), *Kane* (APD-18, UDT-4), and *Clemson* (APD-32, UDT-6), did these recons. The daylight UDT operations, many under fire, were protected by shipboard-mounted 40-mm dual-purpose rapid-fire guns fired overhead by LCIs. Much of the credit for the low casualty rate of such UDTs goes to this close LCI fire support. None of the UDT swimmers ever got out of the surf or actually went inland on any of the selected beaches. Their observations of beach defenses were made from out in the surf and from the reef area. Navy CPO James R. Chittum, a member of UDT 3, confirmed that their observations were made while his team was in the surf, but they were "usually close enough to draw small arms fire."[27]

The major landings were to be done on the western beaches, at Asan, north of the Orote Peninsula, and at Agat, south of the peninsula. The plan was for the two landing forces to turn and form a pincer movement to cut off the peninsula.[28]

On 14 July 1944, UDT 3, commanded by Lt. Thomas C. Crist, USNR, commenced three nights of recon of all selected and several alternate beaches. Beginning at dusk, the UDT swimmers slipped over the sides of their rubber boats and discovered that the Japanese on Guam had prepared antiboat/LVT obstacles in front of all of the usable beaches. Protective overhead fire from battleships, cruisers, destroyers, and LCI gunboats attempted to keep the Japanese heads down while the UDT charted each of the obstacles. Amazingly, UDT 3 lost only one killed during these extensive water recons.[29]

Off Agat, UDT found some 640 obstacles—the most sophisticated antilanding obstacles used by the Japanese to date. Placed in three rows in front of the beaches, they consisted of coconut-log timber "cribs" filled with coral rocks and interconnected with steel cable. Off Asan, enemy engineers had devised concrete cubes consisting of three hundred palm-log frames covered with chicken wire and filled with pieces of coral then filled with cement. Having practiced blowing tetrahedrons off the beaches of Guadalcanal, on 17 July, UDT 4 (Lt. Dearle M. Logsdon, USNR) and UDT 6 (Lt. William Carberry, USNR) began to place charges into the obstacles. The teams completed destruction of all obstacles by the evening of 20 July (W-1). Adding a postscript of levity to this grim operation was the sign audaciously placed at this point on one of the beaches by one of the UDT team members: Welcome Marines! In addition to destruction of the obstacles, Lieutenant Crist's UDT 3 blew a two-hundred-foot channel through the coral. They also blew apart a sunken Japanese vessel that was partially blocking one of the landing force main approach lanes.[30]

Following the pre–W-day preparations, the 3d and 9th Marine Regiments, in Maj. Gen. Allen H. Turnage's 3d Marine Division in the north, stormed ashore on the Asan beaches against strong enemy fire. In the south on the Agat beaches, Brig. Gen. Lem Shepherd's 1st Marine Brigade found even stiffer resistance. Despite the intensive pre–W-day naval gunfire, the southern beaches were dominated by two 75-mm guns and a 37-mm antiboat gun. Before these could be knocked out, twenty-four LVTs were knocked out of action and left as burning hulks on the beaches. This caused later problems in the transfer of men and supplies from the offshore reef. The 1st Provisional Marine Brigade, composed of the 4th Marines and the 22d Marines, after five days of heavy fighting were finally able, on 31 July, to cut off, isolate, and eliminate the four thousand Japanese defenders on the Orote Peninsula.[31]

Capt. Jim Jones's VAC Amphib Recon Battalion was not used for the Guam campaign. As the reader is aware, the recon battalion was just used prior to the Guam landings in Marine operations on Saipan and, most important, Tinian. Other than pre–W-day periscope photography, the only hydrographic reconnaissance was carried out by the UDT teams discussed above.

The 3d Marine Division and the 1st Provisional Marine Brigade each had reconnaissance companies. From close reading of the official history of the 6th Marine Division (which was officially organized immediately after the Guam operation and sprang, as it were, from Maj. Gen. Lem Shepherd's 1st Provisional Marine Brigade), it is clear that Shepherd split the division recon company into its three platoons. He attached one platoon to each of the brigade's regiments, the 4th and 22d: the newly constituted 4th Marines (the original 4th Marines having been taken prisoner in the fall of Corregidor in the Philippines after leaving China) and the 22d Marines (which had previously been a "separate" and independent regiment and had received its blooding on the beaches of Eniwetok; see chap. 7). The 22d's regimental commander, Col. Merlin F. Schneider, kept his regiment's assigned recon platoon close to his command post. Here they were readily available for rapid deployment on recon missions for the regiment. When not being used on specific recon assignments, they were used to help protect the CP.

On the night of W day's landing, General Shepherd and each of his regimental commanders anticipated the usual nightly Japanese counterattacks. Col. Tsunetaro Suenaga, CO of the Japanese 38th Regiment from the elite 29th Division, began his probing attacks at the juncture of the regimental boundaries between the 3d Marine Division's 4th Marines and the Marine Brigade's 22d Marines. After a series of probes beginning at 2130 hours, the enemy charged in force, screaming, carrying their weapons at high port; they overran the forward marine lines and began to penetrate the thinly held Marine rear areas. Star-shell illumination was called for. Marines, evading the Japanese attempts to bayonet them in their fox holes, took a high toll on the attackers. Using grenades, small arms, and mortars, they were able to hold their lines.

One Japanese element of their counterattack force actually made it back to the Marine's 75-mm pack howitzer artillery positions before they were stopped by the gun crews. A Japanese company of infiltrators approached the regimental command post. At this point, the Marine defenders held. Rallying around 1st Lt. Dennis Chavez Jr.'s recon platoon, all hands—clerks, cooks, and supernumeraries—assisted the platoon in stopping the Japanese cold in their tracks. The recon marines quickly exterminated the company. Chavez shot five at point-blank range, using his Thompson submachine gun. The rest were hunted down and shot and, by dawn, the vaunted Japanese 38th Infantry Regiment no longer existed. It was wiped out in this series of savage counterattacks against the 4th and 22d Marine Regiments. Colonel Suenaga was wounded and later killed in these attacks.[32]

Japanese stragglers crept back north to join the reserves in the defense of the high ground around Fonte Ridge above the Asan-Adelup beachhead. In addition to CP defense, Marine and Army recon assets were used in other nonamphibious roles, such as cleanup of bypassed Japanese elements and antisniper patrols. Guam, because of its heavy canopy cover, made ideal terrain for infiltrators and holdouts. Frequently, the first inkling that some of the front-line units would have of an impending counterattack would be when large groups of Japanese would spring forward from the jungle to meet them. Within the 1st Marine Provisional Brigade, on the night of 25–26 July, Colonel Craig was faced with greatly extended frontages on the boundary between his 9th Marines and the adjoining 21st Marines (3d Marine Division). Craig opted to use his Regimental Scout Platoon to help fill this gap between the units. At about 2330, a forward OP reported increased activity in the vicinity of the boundary between the 9th and 21st. At midnight, artillery and mortar fire began to fall in the area. This was the start of another of the major Japanese counterattacks. As a consequence, the lightly armed Regimental Scout Platoon was forced to fall back.[33] Providing OPs and CP defense, and filling gaps as the 9th Marines had, were typical of the division-level utilization of scout platoons. (This contrasts with the deeper corps-level reconnaissance missions such as those carried out by VAC Amphib Recon Battalion.)

A final example of the use of recon assets on Guam was the use of the entire 3d Marine Division Reconnaissance Company with a mechanized reconnaissance-in-force. This was one of the last major actions on Guam and began on 3 August 1944. The 1st Battalion, 9th Marines had secured a series of road junctions below Finegayan Village in the northern sector of Guam. Shortly after noon, "a motorized column was sent out to execute a re-connaissance-in-force ahead of the Division (3rd Mar Div) lines. Plans were to explore the northernmost point of the island- Ritidian Point." The force consisted of the 3d Tank Battalion Headquarters and A Company, 3d Tanks; 3d Marine Division's Reconnaissance Company; and I Company, 21st Marines. The 3d Tank Battalion led out, under their CO, Lt. Col. Hartnoll J. Withers. Cautiously moving generally north and west, two halftracks, two radio jeeps for communication purposes, and one platoon of tanks supported by an infantry platoon moved out just beyond Road Junction 177.

The point of the column was immediately hit by a strong concentration of enemy fire, including 75-mm and 105-mm artillery pieces (firing directly down the road), tanks, mortars, and heavy small-arms and machine-gun fire. The marines, using their tanks, with heavy artillery support, and reinforced by the infantry, returned the assault by fire, and in a matter of just over two hours knocked out the two 75-mm guns, one Japanese tank, and several machine-gun nests. Recognizing that the Japanese held the advantage in both terrain and cover, the reconnaissance-in-force withdrew back through Marine lines, bringing their casualties with them. Marine losses included one halftrack, one six-by-six truck, one tank (damaged), and one officer and twelve marines killed or wounded. It was later determined that this attack had been against a full Japanese battalion of Rikusentai—a Japanese Special Landing Force (Japanese Marines). Rikusentai are considered to be the elite troops within the Japanese forces. Historians later dubbed this reconnaissance-in-force as "the battle of Finegayan."[34]

Following an intense, three-week battle, Guam was finally declared secure on 10 August 1944.

Officers of the first amphibious reconnaissance unit of
the Marine Corps, Amphib Recon Company,
Amphibious Corps, at Camp Catlin, Hawaii, 1943.
Front row: Capt. Jim Jones, Lt. Russ Corey, Lt. Leo
Shinn. *Back row:* Lt. Merwyn Silverthorn Jr., Lt. Harry
Minnear, and Lt. Harvey Weeks.

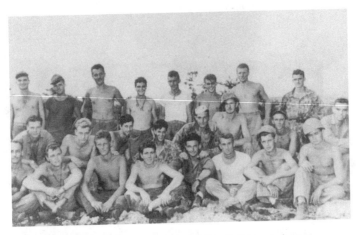

Weapons platoon, B Company, Amphibious Reconnaissance Battalion, VAC, on Saipan, 1944. (Shortly after this photograph was taken, Amphib Recon Battalion, VAC became Amphib Recon Battalion, FMFPac.)

Main Inflation Manifold
Inflation Valves for Pneumatic Deck
Inflation Valves for Cross Tubes
Carbon – Dioxide Bottle
Topping – Off Valve
Machine – Gun Mount Patches
Spray Tube
Spray Tube Valve
Optional Manifold
Motor Mount
Spray Tube Valve
Pelican Hook
Motor-Tool Pocket
Bridle Lines
Life Line
Carrying Handles
Pump Pocket
Towing Howser
Pop-Off Valve
Repair Pockets
Pressure Guage
Quick – Release Line
Motor Mount
Machine – Gun Mount
Carrying Handles
Pelican Hook
Bridle Lines
D-Ring

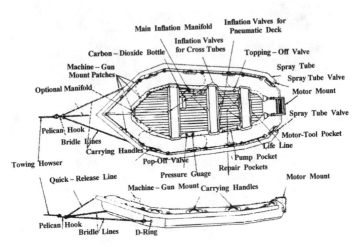

Schematic of a rubber boat (LCR[L]).

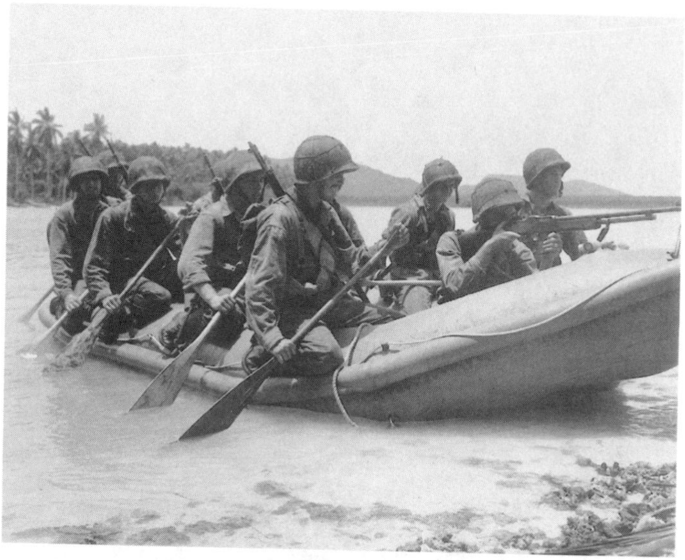

Typical ten-man rubber boat used by Marine amphibious recon, Raiders, Alamo Scouts, and Alaska Scouts in the Pacific theater. Note the BAR on bow.

DOD photo (USMC) 54765, National Archives

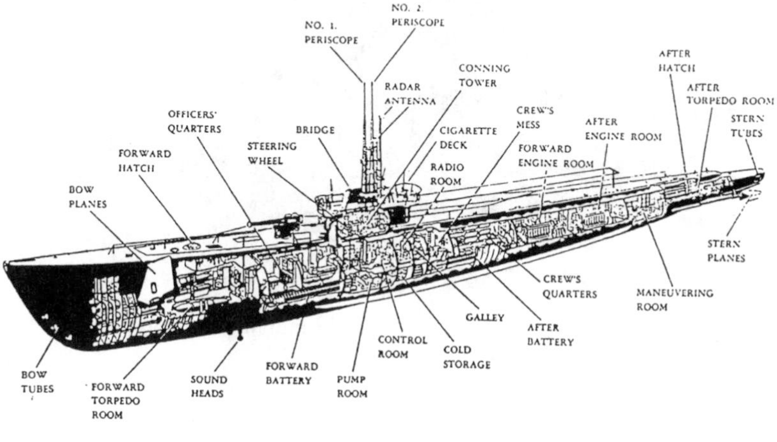

NO. 1. PERISCOPE
NO. 2. PERISCOPE
RADAR ANTENNA
CONNING TOWER
AFTER HATCH
AFTER TORPEDO ROOM
STERN TUBES
OFFICERS' QUARTERS
BRIDGE
CIGARETTE DECK
CREW'S MESS
AFTER ENGINE ROOM
STEERING WHEEL
FORWARD ENGINE ROOM
FORWARD HATCH
RADIO ROOM
BOW PLANES
STERN PLANES
CREW'S QUARTERS
MANEUVERING ROOM
GALLEY
AFTER BATTERY
CONTROL ROOM
COLD STORAGE
FORWARD BATTERY
BOW TUBES
FORWARD TORPEDO ROOM
SOUND HEADS
PUMP ROOM

Schematic of a fleet-class submarine.

Wet-deck launch of rubber boats from the fantail of submarine.
USMC photo A-31994

Dry-deck launch of rubber boats from a fleet-class submarine.

High-speed destroyer transport USS *Dickerson*.
Navy Archives

Typical PT boat used by Marine reconnaissance.
Navy Archives

A PBY Catalina amphibian "Dumbo."
U.S. Navy photo

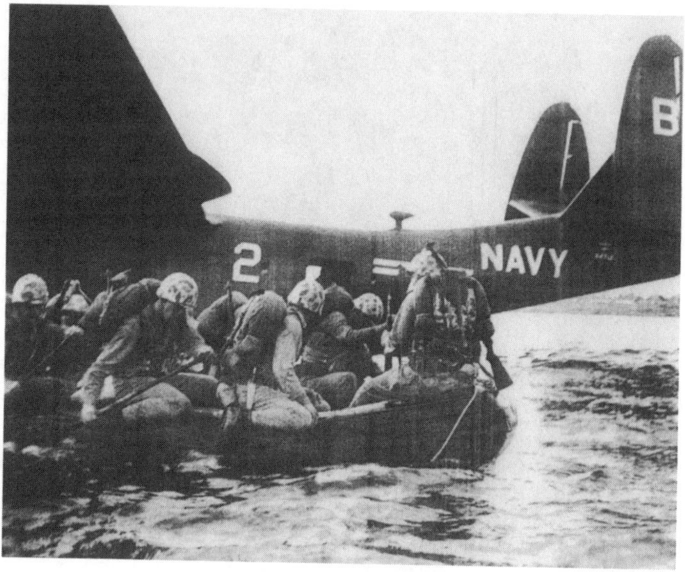
2
NAVY

Recon patrol recovering aboard PBM-5 Martin Mariner.

3d Raider Battalion recon marines stashing their boat in the jungle, just off the beach, Pavuvu, Russell Islands, Solomons, 21 February 1943. This photograph was taken under combat conditions, making it difficult to discern individual marine actions.

National Archives

Native canoe used for Kolambangara Island recon, Solomon Islands, March 1943. Capt. Ed Wheeler is in the bush hat.
USMC photo

1st Lt. Harvey Weeks and PFC C. E. Jung after the taking of Makin Atoll in the Gilbert Islands. PFC Jung was later killed in action in recon actions on Kwajalein.

Japanese naval warrant officer POW, captured by 1st Lt. Harvey Weeks on 1 February 1943 on Majuro Atoll. Here being interrogated by Marine intelligence, aided by Japanese linguists and surrounded by his recon captors aboard USS *Kane*.

Photo courtesy of (former) Cpl. John W. Schiller Jr., USMC, Amphib Recon Battalion, VAC

Amphibious Reconnaissance Battalion officers with B Company officers after Saipan. *Standing, left to right:* CO, Company B, 1st Lt. Leo Shinn; Lt. Merl Gardner; *Seated, left to right:* Battalion CO, 1st Lt. John Burkhard; Lt. Boyce Lassiter; XO, 1st Lt. Russ Corey; Battalion CO, Capt. Jim Jones; Battalion XO, Capt. Earl Marquardt.

Lt. Gen. Holland M. Smith presenting the Legion of Merit to Capt. Jim Jones for the Apamama operation, Gilbert Islands, 1944.

Marine Amphibious Reconnaissance Battalion, FMFPac personnel preparing rubber boats for landings on eastern islands, Okinawa, April 1945.
USMC photo 120002

Marines of the 5th Marine Division Recon Company who carried out the February 1945 D-2 swim onto the beaches of Iwo Jima. The photograph was taken just prior to the operation. *Standing, rear:* Sgt. Cletis E. Peacock, Plt. Sgt. Robert H. Dabney, CO, Capt. Robert G. Reynolds, Sgt. Robert M. Cole, Cpl. Charles L. Linder. *Front, kneeling:* Plt. Sgt. Chester L. Barrett, Sgt. James O. Burns, M.Gy. Sgt. Tony Forte, Cpl. James W. Duncon, and Corporal Thomas (first name unknown).

Photo courtesy of Sgt. James O. Burns, USMC (Ret.)

9

Peleliu and the Palaus

With the seizure of the Marianas, the Joint Chiefs of Staff reviewed their overall strategic planning on the drive across the Pacific. Plans called for two major axes leading to homeland Japan. The first, across the central and western Pacific, the reader has become familiar with. The second was General Douglas MacArthur's moves along the New Guinea–Mindanao axis.[1]

By the summer of 1944, MacArthur's Southwest Pacific drive had taken him to the western tip of New Guinea. U.S. forces on western New Guinea, however, were vulnerable from their northern flank. Some five hundred miles to the north lay the Caroline Islands, more specifically, the Palaus in the western Carolines. The Japanese considered the Palaus of great strategic importance, describing them as the "the spigot of the oil barrel" through which flowed the essential oil taken from the Dutch East Indies.[2]

It was clear to the JCS that the Palaus would have to be taken or neutralized before further moves along either axis. The only way to effectively neutralize this threat to MacArthur's flank would be by amphibious assault. The Palaus run approximately 110 miles north to south, being some 20 miles wide east to west. The island group forms an isosceles triangle, with the island of Peleliu at the apex to the east. Five hundred miles to the southeast, along one leg of the triangle, is New Guinea, 500 miles to the northeast, the other leg of the triangle, is Mindanao. Yap, a large, well-defended airbase island, lies some 240 miles to the east of Peleliu; the JCS believed it could be neutralized with air strikes. In essence, they determined to bypass Yap and leave it to wither on the vine, much the same as several Japanese bases in New Guinea had been bypassed by MacArthur in his move to the western tip of New Guinea.

There were several factors which influenced the Joint Chiefs in their decision to make the Palaus the next target. First, the Palaus offered closer airbases and anchorages for the drive west. Second, Yap's airbases could be neutralized by carrier-air. And finally, the Ulithi Atoll, west of Peleliu, offered the most spacious and pro- tected anchorage in the western Pacific. Once seized, Ulithi could replace the forward fleet anchorage at Eniwetok for rendezvous of necessary shipping for Iwo Jima and Okinawa.[3]

Operation Stalemate II was thus born. Immediately, plan- ning for seizure of Peleliu began. Japanese documents captured on Saipan revealed that Babelthuap, the largest and most northern of the Palaus, was the main bastion of the Japanese defenses, with more than a division of Japanese. The Japanese, anticipating that the Palaus would be the next target in the Pacific, immediately began rapid reinforcement of the islands. The Kwantung Army's 14th Division was brought down from Manchuria.[4] This heavily reinforced Japanese division headquartered on Babelthuap had twenty-five thousand well-trained, well-equipped troops. A heavily reinforced infantry regiment with some ten thousand troops was to defend Peleliu. Japanese defense headquarters was moved from Truk to the Palaus, locating on Babelthuap.[5] Angaur, to the south and west, was to be defended by a reinforced infantry battalion (approximately thirteen hundred troops).

It was decided to bypass the heavily defended Babelthuap, neutralizing it by air strikes, and to seize the two most usable (for airstrips) islands, Peleliu and Angaur. Babelthuap was surrounded by steep cliffs, devoid of any usable beaches, and the island was composed of volcanic, mountainous terrain, covered with thick vegetation. This only confirmed the logic of bypassing Babelthuap. It had only one major airfield. Two islands just to its south, Koror and Arakabesan, contained a seaplane base and a submarine base. Were Peleliu to be seized, with its relatively good airfield, both these bases would effectively be neutralized.

Peleliu, at the southern end of the Palaus, had some good beaches but also had a wide barrier reef on the west, where more accommodating beaches were located. A fringing reef to the east

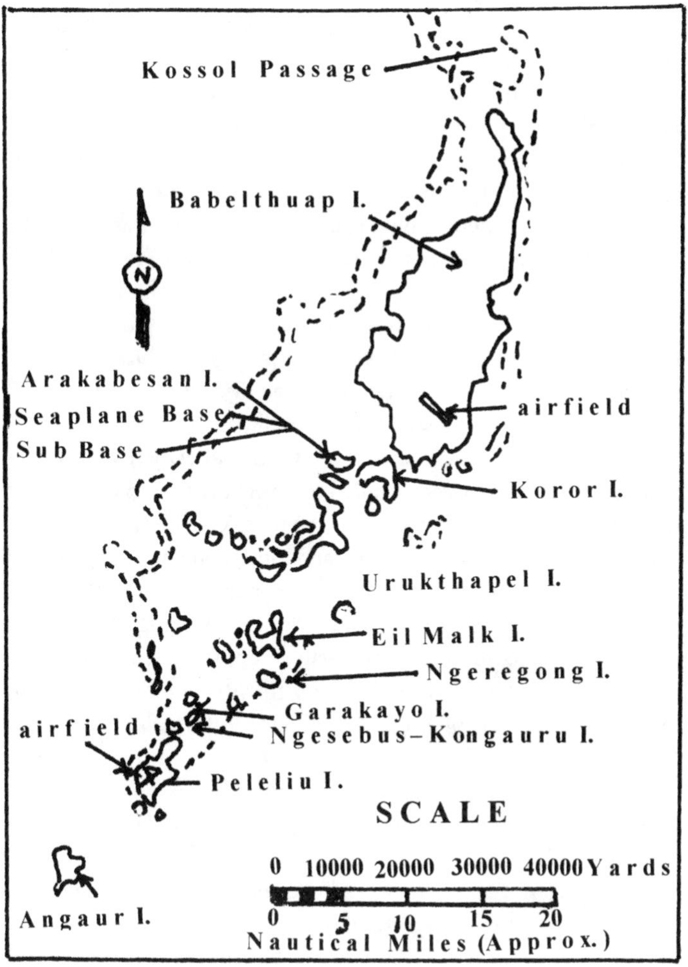
Kossol Passage
Babelthuap I.
N
Arakabesan I.
Seaplane Base
Sub Base
airfield
Koror I.
Urukthapel I.
Eil Malk I.
Ngeregong I.
Garakayo I.
airfield
Ngesebus-Kongauru I.
Peleliu I.
SCALE
0 10000 20000 30000 40000 Yards
0 5 10 15 20
Nautical Miles (Approx.)
Angaur I.

The Palau Islands
Courtesy of the History and Museums Division, HQMC

mitigated against a landing on the east. A landing on the western beaches would, however, entail transfers to amphibious tractors and DUKWs at the reef edge and require crossing this wide open lagoon area, susceptible to artillery and mortar defensive fire and antiboat guns. Peleliu is just six-by-two miles in size, shaped somewhat like a lobster claw's pincers. One of the "claws" to the south tapered off in swamps and sharp coral. It was flat on the southern end, rising north of the airfield in a series of limestone and coral ridges that had been heaved up to form a series of compartments and cross-compartments which would prove deadly to seize. This terrain was laced with natural caves, and the Japanese had imported mining and tunnel engineers to perfect even deadlier defensive positions there. The massif along the ridge was called the Umurbrogol; the Japanese name for this terrain was Momoji.[6] Both Peleliu and Angaur, the southernmost islands in the Palaus, had been developed for their phosphates and copra. A phosphate refinery on the northern tip of Peleliu was connected to two small, relatively flat islands both interconnected by causeways to Peleliu.[7]

The United States had little intelligence on Peleliu, other than fairly accurate estimates as to the number of Japanese defenders. Aerial photography failed to reveal the true magnitude of the Umurbrogol ridges, with their steep peaks, cliffs, and box canyons. This less-than-optimum aerial photography was due to cloud cover, heavy jungle growth, and clever Japanese camouflage and concealment of their defensive installations. During the later assault, this shortcoming in intelligence bore tragic consequences. The Umurbrogol was covered by scrub growth, and the aerial photo interpreters did not pick up this extremely difficult and broken terrain.

Having been set back because the actions on Guam had taken longer than anticipated, D-day was finally set for 15 September 1944.

Intelligence on Peleliu's beaches came almost exclusively from photographs. Pre–D-day periscope photography was done by the submarine *Seawolf,* under Lt. Cdr. A. M. Bontier, between 4 and 7 July 1944 and provided some assault views that proved helpful.[8] Later that summer, between 11 and 20 August, *Burrfish,* under Lt. Cdr. W. B. Perkins, made similar periscope photos of both Peleliu and Angaur for the coordinated secondary seizure of Angaur by the Army's 81st Division.[9] No pre–D-day amphibious reconnaissance was used at Peleliu. Having said that, one would think that with the thrust of this book being amphibious reconnaissance, that would end my description of the campaign. On the contrary, because of the lack of amphibious reconnaissance, it is appropriate to discuss Peleliu, arguably because of some of the consequences of conducting an assault landing without amphib recon.

In retrospect, it appears obvious that Generals Geiger (CG, III Amphibious Corps) and Rupertus (CG, 1st Marine Division) made the decision not to use amphib recon because of the very heavily defended beaches and because there was no need for the element of surprise in the precise location of the landings, since fleet bombardment had already commenced on D-3. Colonel Williams, in his excellent analytical review of these landings, pointed out that on Saipan and Guam, little attempt was made at deception as to which beaches were to be used and, as a result, the beaches were bloody. The Japanese defenders knew exactly where we were to land, and they massed their mobile artillery and mortars accordingly. On Tinian, the recon was done in a clandestine manner, and excellent diversionary operations were conducted in other locations to mask the surreptitious and highly successful entry of recon personnel onto the beaches to be used by the landing force. This resulted in minimal casualties during the actual landing.[10]

Despite the fact that Marine recon personnel were not employed before D-day because of concerns for security, UDT teams did yeoman service on their one pre–D-day beach recon and their other demolition operations. Lt. E. C. Kirkpatrick, USN, Lt. (jg) M. R. Massie, and nine UDT team members went ashore from *Burrfish* in two rubber boats on the night of 11 August 1944, actually landing on one of the Peleliu beaches later used in the assault.[11] Unfortunately, their attention was only directed to the characteristics of the beach itself; consequently, they gained no knowledge of the defenses just behind the beaches or of the antiboat guns at either ends of the beaches. Lieutenant Kirkpatrick's report aptly describes their activities:

> The *Burrfish* reached the vicinity of Peleliu on 30 Jul 1944 but because of the bright moonlight the first landing was not attempted until the night of 11 August, when one of the beaches of Peleliu was reconnoitered. Much valuable information was obtained, indicating that LVTs, DUKWs and possibly LCTs could be used for landings on that particular

beach but that smaller landing craft would have difficulty because of surf conditions. Further [UDT] landing party reconnaissance on the other beaches of Peleliu or on the beaches of Angaur were prevented by the intensity of Jap radar activity, and on 14 August *Burrfish* proceeded to Yap.[12]

After delivering their beach data and Burrfish's periscope photos to their fellow submarine *Balao* for quick delivery to Pearl Harbor, the UDT team continued aboard *Burrfish* to reconnoiter the island of Gagil Tomil on Yap Atoll. Unfortunately, three (four, according to Morison) of the UDT who went ashore on the night of 18–19 August in their recon on Yap were either killed or captured and were never recovered.[13]

Unlike in the Solomons, Gilberts, and Marshalls, there were no former tourists, traders, or Coastwatchers in the Palaus who could provide intelligence. The landing would have to go forward strictly on the periscope photography and the poor quality aerial photography. The loss of UDT men in their beach recon on Ulithi reinforced the prior decision that any inland reconnaissance was impossible, precluded by the known heavily defended Peleliu.[14]

Three days before D-day on Peleliu, when the landing was to begin, the irrepressible Admiral Halsey, swayed by lack of opposition to his forays along the Philippines (on 13 September 1944), suggested canceling the seizures of Peleliu, Angaur, and Yap-Ulithi. He recommended bypassing them, instead going directly into an invasion of Leyte and Samar.[15] This recommendation was quickly rejected by Admiral Nimitz and the JCS, who felt that the southern Palaus were essential for advance bases before Leyte could be seized.[16]

The III Amphibious Corps, led by Maj. Gen. Roy Geiger, tasked Maj. Gen. William H. Rupertus's 1st Marine Division for the main assault landings on Peleliu. The Army's 81st Infantry Division (Maj. Gen. Paul J. Mueller) was assigned to later seize Angaur, with initial assignment of one of its regimental combat teams (RCTs) as a reserve for the Peleliu landing. Angaur was to be taken next, after Peleliu.

As mentioned, the UDT's planned pre–D-day beach recon in July and August had been all but truncated by the moonlit nights and heavy Japanese radar, air, and sea patrols. *Burrfish* had been kept submerged for two weeks, limited to periscope photography, except for the one night, and very brief, surf, reef, and beachfront rubber-boat reconnaissance.

Once the western beaches had been chosen as the landing beaches, more detailed information on the beaches and reef was going to have to wait until just before D-day. At 0530 hours on 12 September 1944, naval gunfire and, later, air strikes began to fall on the beaches and inland. Initially, only two days of naval gunfire had been scheduled, but upon insistence of the landing force, this was extended to three days. Nevertheless, this proved, in hindsight, to be insufficient.

At 1030, two APDs closed the western reef off Orange and White Beaches, landing two UDT teams (veterans of Guam and Saipan UDT ops) by rubber boat. They located and marked the boulders and coral heads, and they mined wooden obstacles that were to be taken out the next day (D-2). This recon and the following day's actual demolitions were done under the cover of 40-mm suppressing fire from LCIs. Despite this suppressive fire, several casualties were taken by UDT from small-arms, machine-gun, and mortar fire.

The evening of 14–15 September, Japanese "stealth swimmers" came out onto the reef and planted a series of horned mines, just 150 yards off the landing beaches. In their haste, fortunately for the marine landing forces, these Japanese swimmers failed to pull the safety pins on the mines and they did not activate during the landing.[17]

The 1st Marine Division Reconnaissance Company, initially as part of the "floating reserve," was ordered ashore by the division commander, Major General Rupertus, early in the afternoon of D-day. He had them land in Col. Herman Hanneken's 7th Marines' zone of action. Hannekan had reported "heavy casualties" and requested ammo and reinforcements. One experienced operations officer and infantry unit commander, Col. Tom Fields, later wrote that, in his opinion, ordering the unit in "as infantry replacements" was "an improper use of the Reconnaissance Company, as there later developed several opportunities for employment of this company in the manner for which it had been trained," for example, on the causeways to the north.[18] I concur with Colonel Fields. Other examples of the misuse of trained recon personnel have been explored in previous chapters. For the most part, this misuse has been at the Marine division level, that is, with the Scouts and Snipers, recon platoons, or, as in this case, an entire division recon company.

Additional proof of the use of these recon troops as "line fillers" or plain replacements is given in two letters to the Historical Division of HQMC. One was by Lt. Col. John Ghormley, then CO 1st Battalion, 7th Marines, who recalled that the recon company had been deployed behind the lines of 1/7 on the night of D-day. This was affirmed in a postwar letter to HQMC by 1st Lt. Robert L. Powell Jr., who was commanding the 2d Platoon of the Division Recon Company. He received a request from Ghormley to "move forward and plug the lines" (of 1/7). They did this, filling a "gap" in 1/7's lines during the expected Japanese counterattack against the landing beach. The platoon "accounted for at least 30 of the enemy killed during the night."[19]

The landings on Peleliu were deadly and costly. The assault waves, landing entirely by LVT, were heavily hit by antiboat guns at the flanks of all beaches and by artillery and heavy mortars from masked terrain behind the beaches. Peleliu proved to be a benchmark in the defensive tactics by the Japanese. This was to be replicated in spades in the next landings on Iwo Jima and Okinawa. In sum, the Japanese on Peleliu built their MLR well back from the beaches so that it would not be knocked out at the outset by naval gunfire and air strikes, which were concentrated on the immediate landing beaches. In addition, sufficient reserves were held back for massive counterattacks. Their defenses on Peleliu were carefully integrated and mutually supporting. Defenses were much more in-depth, and terrain was skillfully utilized to provide the Japanese with greater flexibility than afforded in earlier island defenses against assault landings.[20] As a consequence, casualties were higher in the assault forces. The fighting lasted nearly ten weeks and cost nearly 10,000 U.S. casualties (3,089 Army, 6,526 Marine). Of these casualties, 1,252 were killed in action.[21]

Angaur, a flatter island than Peleliu, was taken by the Army's 81st Division with, compared to Peleliu, fairly modest casualties.

During the operation, which started with the landings on F day, 17 September 1944, and concluding on 14 October 14, the Army lost a total 260 killed in action and 1,354 wounded in action. They killed 1,338 Japanese and captured 59 POWs.[22] I found no independent references to describe the Army's use of its reconnaissance assets during this operation.

In conclusion, the Marines suffered heavy casualties against a well-entrenched enemy on the more-mountainous Peleliu. All of the histories on the Peleliu campaign recount the extreme difficulties the 1st Marine Division faced in this bloody assault. Of particular note was the eventual surrounding and final overcoming of the Umurbrogol ridges, primarily by Col. Lewis B. "Chesty" Puller's 1st Marine Regiment. Puller's marines were later relieved by elements of both Colonel Hanneken's 7th Marines as well as the Army's 321st Infantry Regiment of the 81st Division. A very high proportion of the 1st Marines' leaders were killed or wounded. (Although not wounded on Peleliu, Puller suffered painfully there from his earlier severe wounding on Guadalcanal.) These heavy casualties were stark testimony to both the skill of the Japanese defenders and the consummate combat skill of the marines and soldiers who eventually took the Umurbrogol.[23]

10

The Volcano Islands and Iwo Jima

The ring began to further tighten on homeland Japan. The overall "grand strategy," which had been outlined at the "Octagon" conference in September 1944 between Roosevelt, Churchill, and their Combined Joint Chiefs of Staff, began to be implemented. The seizure of the Marianas generally went according to schedule, only Guam taking longer than anticipated. When Peleliu in the Palau Islands was seized in October 1944, it also took longer than initially projected. With MacArthur's landings on Leyte in October 1944, modifications to the JCS directive now appeared necessary. The initial directive called for (1) MacArthur to seize Luzon with a target date of December 1944, and (2) Nimitz, after providing cover and support for the Luzon operation, to seize one or more islands in the Bonins or Volcano Islands on or about 20 January 1945, with seizure of Okinawa in the Ryukus on or about 1 March. Both Formosa and Amoy, because of their physical size, proximity to Japanese air strikes, and large numbers of Japanese defenders, were to be bypassed.[1]

Iwo Jima, rather than ChiChi Jima, 145 miles farther west, was selected by Nimitz. The largest of the Volcano Islands, Iwo Jima was just 670 miles south of Tokyo and was nearly the halfway point (between our new bases in the Marianas and Tokyo) for B-29 bombings scheduled for the home islands. The island was also 625 miles north of the newly acquired Saipan-Tinian B-29 bases. When seized, it would have the added plus of providing airfields for P-51 Mustangs to escort the B-29s to Tokyo.[2]

As the most heavily fortified island in the Japanese defenses, the campaign for Iwo Jima would prove to be the bloodiest and costliest in Marine Corps history. The Japanese had deduced that we were coming next to Iwo and thus began to bring in the 109th Infantry Division as reinforcement. The emperor himself designated Lt. Gen. Tadamichi Kuribayashi as his commander on Iwo. Kuribayashi was a brilliant cavalry officer. He was battle-hardened and had taken part in the seizure of Hong Kong. He was an excellent staff officer and the emperor had great trust in him (justifiably so from the results that he achieved during the defense of Iwo Jima).[3]

The delays caused by the support of Luzon and the seizures of Saipan, Tinian, and Guam and later Peleliu gave the Japanese a window of opportunity to further reinforce Iwo. They took full advantage and brought in much heavier beach-defense weapons, artillery, tanks, and many more troops. At the time of the assault by U.S. forces, the Japanese had approximately twenty-one thousand officers and men on the island.[4]

Iwo Jima, which means "sulfur island" in Japanese, is a small, pear-shaped volcanic island in the Volcano Island chain. It runs four and a half miles northeast-southwest and is two and a quarter miles wide at its northern end and half a mile wide at its southern end. There are numerous deposits of yellow sulfur, overlain with black volcanic ash and sand, on the island and very little vegetation (primarily a few gnarled trees and sea grasses). Iwo has no natural water, no rivers or lakes, so potable water is either imported by tankers or rainwater caught in cisterns. In the south is Mount Suribachi, 550 feet high with steep sides all around. The terrain rises gradually as one moves north on the island, and there is a hilled plateau at the northern tip which varies from 300 to 500 hundred feet in elevation. The island's entire north end is ringed by steep, volcanic cliffs that run down to the sea. At the time of the assault, the only usable beaches were one on the western part of the southern end, north of Suribachi, and one on the southeast side of the main airfield (the "eastern" beaches). Both of these beaches have a very steep gradient, and the plunging surf breaks very close to the shoreline, making it hazardous for small craft. Two large rocky/volcanic islands sit to the west of Iwo, Kangoku Rock and Kama Rock. Off the eastern beaches, about midbeach, there is a rocky promontory called Futatsu Rock.

The battle of Iwo Jima, code named Operation Detachment, has been extensively written about, so I will discuss only briefly

Kangoku Rock
Kama Rock
Airfield # 3
Airfield # 2
Airfield # 1
Western Beaches
Eastern Beaches
Futatsu Rock
Mt. Suribachi
Tobiishi Pt.
IWO JIMA
500
0
1200
yards

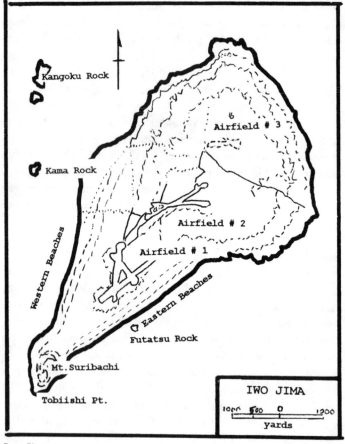

Iwo Jima
Courtesy of the History and Museums Division, HQMC

and in general terms the units and the tactical situation. Readers who are interested in a more in-depth discussion of the battle should look to any of the excellent treatises on this subject.

Overall command for the operation was given by Admiral Nimitz to Admiral Spruance, who commanded the Fifth Fleet. Second in operational command was Rear Adm. Harry Hill. As CG, FMFPac, Lt. Gen. H. M. Smith was given the title of CG, Expeditionary Troops, while Maj. Gen Harry Schmidt was given the title "Commander of the Landing Force." The landing force was composed of the 3d, 4th, and 5th Marine Divisions, commanded respectively by Maj. Gens. Graves B. Erskine, Clifton B. Cates, and Keller E. Rockey. Both the 3d and 4th Divisions had been well blooded (the 3d at Bougainville and Guam, the 4th at Roi-Namur and Saipan/Tinian). For the 5th Marine Division, Iwo was going to be the first and only major battle as a division during World War II. Formed at Camp Pendleton in November 1943, it shipped out to Hawaii in August 1944. In Hawaii, it worked closely with the more experienced 4th Division. Over half of the enlisted in the newly formed 5th Division had seen combat in prior tours with other units. While in Hawaii, it landed on beaches with soft volcanic sand and maneuvered on a hill somewhat resembling Mount Suribachi.[5]

The tactical plan was straightforward: the 4th and 5th Marine Divisions were to land abreast on the eastern beaches (weather and surf permitting) and the 3d Marine Division, as the Expeditionary Troops Reserve, was, when released, to land in trace over the same beaches as the assault divisions. Despite entreaties for ten days of naval gunfire, the planners and senior naval commanders allocated only three days for preassault bombardment. Everyone from General Smith down felt that three days was woefully inadequate and, in hindsight, contributed greatly to the very high casualties sustained. This has led to acrimonious criticism in any discussions of the battle in postwar and war college analyses. General Smith discusses this at some length in his memoirs, *Coral and Brass.*[6]

Lt. Gen. Millard F. Harmon, U.S. Army Air Corps, as CG Air Forces Pacific, commenced daily B-29 raids on Iwo which ran for some seventy-five days prior to the landing. He had aerial photos taken which were made into maps for the assault and for aerial photo interpretation. The Japanese had done a masterful job of camouflage and artfully used the terrain to hide pillboxes and defensive gun positions. Despite the extensive aerial photography, limited aerial photographic interpretation (API) intelligence was gained before the assault, quantitatively less intelligence than on most of the previous amphibious landings in the Pacific.[7]

The submarine *Spearfish,* Cdr. G. C. Cole, conducted photographic reconnaissance of Iwo Jima and Minami Jima between

28 November and 2 December 1944. As an addition to the by-now-usual periscope photography for the assault forces, they took pictures of the PPI scope showing the offshore islands. (The PPI, or plan position indicator, displays the position of the ship in relation to surrounding waters, headlands, islands, and so on.) This would augment information for the making up of special sea-area charts for the naval gunfire ships operating areas and for landing craft control vessels near the line of departure.[8]

There are several noteworthy amphibious reconnaissance incidents that took place at Iwo Jima. Many involved B Company, VAC Amphib Recon Battalion. The bulk of the pre–D-day recon of the main landing beaches, however, was done by the recon companies of both the 4th and 5th Marine Divisions. As previously noted, they were augmented by three marines from B Company, VAC Amphib Recon Battalion.

Following their successful employments on Saipan and the Tinian recon, the VAC Amphibious Reconnaissance Battalion had returned from Tinian on the *Azalea City* to Pearl Harbor and their base at Camp Catlin. In January, the battalion was alerted to send one of their companies to Iwo Jima, while the remainder of the battalion (less B Company) was alerted for employment on the forthcoming Okinawa operation.

1st Lt. Russell Corey's B Company, VAC Amphib Recon Battalion embarked on the *Bladen* (APA 63) and took part in the rehearsals around Hawaii for the Iwo landings. Corey (now brigadier general) recently advised me that these were more like floating CPXs (command-post exercises) and he did not remember their actual embarkation in their rubber boats during these 16–24 January rehearsals.[9] Three days later, Corey's company departed for Iwo, arriving off the island on 18 February. They had been alerted to do the pre–D-day amphib recon of the landing beaches, but this mission was canceled for the entire company at the last minute. In Hawaii, Corey been tasked to detach three of his recon marines for attachment to a composite group of marine recon and UDT. Two marine officers and twenty enlisted were formed from the recon platoons from the 4th and 5th Marine Divisions as well as the three recon marines from B Company, VAC Amphib Recon Battalion into a "provisional amphibious reconnaissance unit."

Apparently, this was done to expedite passage and briefing of the firsthand intelligence information from their beach recons to their respective parent regimental staffs. This twenty-two-marine recon unit embarked at Pearl Harbor on the *Blessman* (APD 48). For Iwo Jima, four UDT teams (12, 13, 14, and 15), augmented by this twenty-two-marine unit, were to do the pre–D-day amphib recon of both the eastern and western beaches. Four APDs, the *Bull, Bates, Barr,* and *Blessman,* took nearly one hundred UDT and recon marines to just off the eastern landing beaches on the morning of D-2 (17 February 1945). This was an unusual day-light recon of the approaches and the beaches that were to be used in the assault on D-day. The landings had been preceded by minesweeping, which commenced at 0700 hours. Naval gunfire bombardment by the battleships *Idaho, Nevada,* and *Tennessee* commenced as the BBs closed to three thousand yards. The cruiser *Pensacola* observed the Japanese batteries open fire on the mine-sweepers. *Pensacola* took six hits in this exchange and silenced the offending batteries within five minutes.

At 1025 on D-2, Rear Admiral Blandy, commander Am-phibious Support Forces, ordered the fire-support ships to retire to clear the approach lanes for UDT and marine recons at 1100 hours. The *Barr, Bates, Blessman,* and *Bull* had slowed and dropped their Higgins boats, with the crew of each landing craft personnel ramped (LCP[R]) immediately lashing a rubber boat to their star-board sides. They started their run to the beach with UDTs and marines embarked.

The minesweeping completed, the LCP-Higgins boats passed through the line of twelve landing craft infantry gunboats (LCI[G]) about seven hundred yards off the eastern beaches. The Higgins boats, rubber boats lashed to their sides, made their runs to some three hundred yards off the beaches. They began to drop their swimmers (both UDT and Marine). Because the waters off Iwo are very cold in February, some of the swimmers (mostly UDT) had covered themselves with a thick coat of Navy water pump grease (at the time, there were no cold-water or exposure suits).[10]

Despite the intensive and continuous series of B-29 raids, and the naval gunfire from the five BBs, it was not until the morn-ing of D-2, when the LCI(G)s began firing their 20-mms, 40-mms, and 4.5-inch rockets over the heads of the UDT and marine recon swimmers in the water, that the Japanese began firing. General Kuribayashi, mistakenly sensing that this was the main invasion, "opened up" with his heretofore hidden gun positions. The APDs, with recon and UDT aboard, had actually circled Iwo only the day before (D-3) and had not received any fire. The marines were hopeful, but also realistic, and were not surprised at their reception on D-2.

Unlike any other of the Pacific island recons, a new, "additional" mission of this recon was to "try to draw the fire of the Japanese to get them to expose their gun positions."[11] Each of the three Higgins Boats had a recon team aboard (two scout-swimmer/hydrographers and a photographer); all crouched as low as possible to avoid being hit. They began closing to within two to three hundred yards, making zigzag runs parallel to the invasion beaches. First over the side went the recon swimmers and UDT. The recon photographers, who remained on the Higgins boats, began taking photos of each of the beach defenses. The Japanese fired at them continually, using light mortars, machine guns, and rifle fire as well as the very devastating antiboat guns from their concealed positions. The close splashes and water plumes of the Japanese antiboat guns and mortars, sometimes bracketing their craft, gave everyone a great deal of concern.

Rear Admiral Morison described a portion of this anti–boat/ship fire: "A heavy battery, casemated at the foot of Mt. Suribachi joined in . . . [and] the heaviest fire came from a hitherto unrevealed battery in the high ground, just north of the beaches."[12] Upon completion of the recon/UDT swimmers' missions, the swimmers were picked up using the ring over the upraised arm, the speed of the landing craft pulling them in to the rubber boats. Swimmers aboard, the Higgins boats quickly made for the gunboats. Fighters came in low at about this time, laying smoke, and the DDs fired white phosphorous (WP) shells to cover their withdrawal.[13] Every one of the twelve LCI(G)s had been hit or was sinking. The incredible bravery of these men was noteworthy.

Finding the LCI(G) 466 still afloat and operating, the recon marines went aboard and exited the beach area. While aboard 466,

Sgt. Jim Burns, a recon photographer, and an accompanying UDT liaison officer, Ens. Frank Jirka, were both hit with shrapnel, Burns in his arm, torso, and eye, Jirka in his legs. The Japanese had obviously been firing blindly through the smoke. They and the other wounded were brought alongside the *Tennessee* for lifesaving surgery and later evacuation. After being hit, Burns turned his Contax camera and its precious film over to Captain Reynolds for use in briefing the commanders. Jirka, unfortunately, lost both legs. Burns was med-evacced to Hawaii and then to the States. He later received the Bronze Star for his actions.[14]

The eastern beaches were covered photographically (left to right) by Sergeant Burns (with Captain Reynolds aboard) on Green Beach under the southeastern corner of Suribachi, Sgt. Clete Peacock covered Red Beach 1 in the center, and Sgt. Robert Cole covered Red Beach 2 on the right (Futatsu Rock separated Red 1 from Red 2). Peacock and Burns both had Contax 35-mm cameras, and Cole had a Leica.[15] The recon company of the 4th Marine Division was simultaneously doing identical recons and photography with their UDT teams on the more eastern beaches, Yellow 1 and 2 and Blue 1 and 2.

Late on the afternoon of D-2, the same recon/UDT groups (less the casualties of the morning eastern beach recons) did the western beaches—Brown 1 and 2, White 1 and 2, and Orange 1 and 2—commencing at 1630. The swimmers again entered the water and checked for mines and underwater obstacles, and the marines carried out the beach hydrography. The last UDT/Marine recon swimmer was back aboard by 1800. Upon their return to their command ships to brief the commanders, the beach photography, albeit saltwater streaked and soaked, proved to be invaluable. The landing force commanders, each division and each regimental commander, were briefed at this time. The photos were most helpful in targeting for the final bombardments prior to the landing. They also alerted commanders from where they could expect fire once on the beaches.[16]

This is a classic example of how all elements of recon come together to assist the landing force commanders in reaching appropriate decisions based upon the latest intelligence. At Iwo, unlike many recons in previous operations, photography from the water's edge gave an added plus to this complex matrix we call military intelligence.

The three marines under Sergeant Holland from B Company, VAC Amphib Recon Battalion remained with their UDT counterparts aboard the APD *Blessman*. Collectively, the UDTs and marines reported that they found only one mine off the western beaches, and that was blown. There were no minefields or underwater obstacles on either the eastern or western beaches. Between the marines and the UDTs, sufficient beach data with respect to gradients and surf conditions were obtained to permit the later scheduled D-day landings two days hence.

With its UDT/marine recon swimmers aboard, *Blessman* departed the beach area to close with and rejoin Rear Admiral Rogers's Gunfire and Covering Force offshore. A two-plane enemy air raid developed about 2130 hours, and the APD *Blessman* and destroyer-minesweeper *Gamble* were hit. The aircraft made a stern approach on *Blessman,* dropping a bomb that passed down through its forward troop spaces hitting the forward fireroom below. The ship suffered extensive damage, and forty-two men aboard were killed or missing, twenty-nine wounded in action. Among those killed was B Company, VAC Amphib Recon Battalion's Sgt. Melvin C. Holland. Despite their daring swimming and short beach incursion earlier in the day, fate caught up with the recon marines and others in the brave crew on the *Blessing.*[17]

First Lieutenant Corey's B Company, VAC Amphib Recon Battalion's 125 marines and 6 officers landed late by LCVP, after dark, during the evening of D+1. There were not many marines on the beach at the time of their landing; most had moved short distances inland for the night. Corey remembered not wishing to risk being shot by nervous fellow marines: "We dug into the steep volcanic sand, just short of the berm line above us. It was cold, misty and damp and we had landed only in our utility uniforms. Sympathetic Navy coxswains gave some of my marines their foul-weather jackets and literally stripped off their wool blue pullover sweaters for us." Despite this added gear, most marines were still cold and miserable this first night ashore on Iwo. "At dawn we awoke to the debris and confusion on the beach: wrecked landing craft, burned-out LVTs, supplies and ammunition piling up, waiting to go inland, dead marines waiting to be evacuated, we faced a confusing array of debris present during assault landing."[18]

Finding a knowledgeable beachmaster, Lieutenant Corey and his company moved out to the west toward Suribachi. They were quickly put into the perimeter lines with the 28th Marines near the base of the mountain, where they stayed for a number of days. Corey began reporting in daily to the CP, which was located inland, farther to the north. The CP, recon, and the advance party had landed on D+4 (23 February 1945). Corey told me how his recon marines had brought their dog, Lady, a shepherd mix, from Hawaii. She was not an "official" war dog, more of a pet of the loving marines who had smuggled her along on the accommodating troop transport. While they were with the 28th Marines in the Mount Suribachi area, awaiting assignment of a recon mission, they took daily mortar fire into their lines. Along with some of the recon marines, Lady was wounded by the mortar shrapnel. The corpsman was able to nurse her through to recovery, and she later made the Okinawa operation, ending her war with both "Iwo and Okinawa and a purple heart."[19] While on this duty, B Company had the opportunity to observe the flag raising on 23 February. Later, they watched the landing of the first crippled B-29 on the still-damaged airfield.[20]

On about 11 March 1945, some three weeks after landing B Company, VAC Amphib Recon Battalion was given the mission of landing on and conducting a recon of the two major islands just off the northwestern coast of Iwo Jima, Kama Rock and Kangoku Rock. Some of the marines advancing up the west coast had felt that they had received fire from seaward in the vicinity of these rocks. Other marines, and Navy beachmasters, felt that the Japanese had Coastwatchers on these rocks who helped adjust fire on shipping approaching the western beaches during the early weeks of the campaign.

Lieutenant Corey and B Company boarded twelve amphibious tractors from the 2d Armored Amphibious Tractor Battalion (Amtrac Battalion). Riding on top of these floating artillery pieces, they landed on Kama Rock and found no evidence of Japanese occupation. Boarding their LVT(A)s again, they moved north to Kangoku Rock, the larger island. Here they did find some stone emplacements and caves which evidenced Japanese activity. With this negative report, they reboarded their amtracs and returned to Iwo.[21]

Upon return to VAC Corps field headquarters on Iwo, they found a message from their battalion commander, Maj. Jim Jones, who was with the remainder of the Amphib Recon Battalion in Hawaii. It directed B Company to proceed to Saipan for R&R, there to reequip and get ready for their operations on Okinawa. In Jones's terse message, nothing was said as to how or by what ship, only to "proceed without delay." Corey, exercising his own initiative, made his way down to the beach where they had landed and sought out the beachmaster. "I have 6 marine officers and 125 marines and have to get them to Saipan," he said. As vessels came in to offload on the beach, he would hail them and inquire about their plans and destinations. Finally, he located an LST skipper who was backloading damaged LVTs for transport to Saipan for repair. LST 784 obliged him with a run to Saipan. The marines arrived three days later (19 March 1945) and began replacing their damaged gear, relaxing in this now "rear area." While en route to Saipan on the LST, word came down that Iwo Jima had been declared secure on the twenty-sixth.[22]

11

The Ryukyu Islands and Okinawa

The Ryukyu Islands lie almost midway down the 790-mile arc of islands running from the southern homeland island of Kyushu to Formosa (Taiwan). Okinawa is nearly at the center of the Ryukyus. The island proper covers an area of 485 square miles, 60 miles north to south and 18 miles at its widest, narrowing to 2.5 miles at the Ishikawa Isthmus at the base of the upper third. The northern third of the island is mountainous and heavily wooded, covered with scrub and junglelike growth. The center is hilly in parts, with many paddies and fields that, before the war, were planted with sweet potatoes, sugar cane, and rice, the main cash crops. The two best harbors, Hagushi Anchorage and Nakagusuku (later to be renamed Buckner Bay in honor of Lt. Gen. Simon Bolivar Buckner), and the three major airfields, Yontan, Kadena, and Naha, lie within the southern half of the island. The lower one-third reverts to volcanic and tumbled limestone and coral cliffs cut in a series of steep ridges and canyons. The main island of Okinawa is at the center of some fifty smaller islands of varying sizes in the Okinawa Islands.[1]

The operation to seize Okinawa was given the code name Iceberg. Adm. Ernest King, Adm. Chester Nimitz, the Army's Lt. Gen. Simon Bolivar Buckner, commander of landing forces, and Lt. Gen. Millard "Miff" Harmon of the Army Air Corps met in San Francisco for finalization of the invasion plans. L day was tentatively set for 1 April 1945. Okinawa would prove to be one of the longer operations in the central and South Pacific. It was also the most costly, involving six divisions and almost six times the naval shipping of Guadalcanal, even though actual conflict lasted three-plus months for Okinawa versus nearly five months for Guadalcanal. The field army, commanded by Lieutenant General Buckner, was divided into two corps: the III Amphibious Corps, consisting of the 1st, 2d, and 6th Marine Divisions, and the Army's XXIV Corps, consisting of the 7th, 77th, and 96th Divisions. The heroism and sacrifices the Navy, which lost on average one and a half ships a day, made Okinawa also the costliest of naval involvements in the history of sea warfare.[2]

Anticipating eventual invasion of the home islands of Japan, Admiral King had reluctantly agreed to Nimitz and Turner's reasoning that we needed Okinawa and its two excellent harbors to be the assembly and launching site for eventual invasion of the homeland. Several historians have likened our need for Okinawa to our use of England as a forward staging/launch area for the Normandy invasion.[3]

With the shock of our seizure of Saipan and Tinian, the Japanese general staff were given a ten-month "window," from September 1944 until the invasion, in which to increase Japanese troop strength on Okinawa from 11,000 to 155,000. The Japanese Thirty-second Army, under Lt. Gen. Mitsuru Ushijima, had been reinforced with heavy mortar and artillery as well as tank and antitank units. Despite the almost 60 percent destruction of Japanese shipping by U.S. submarines, Okinawa added to its defensive numbers with use of the native Okinawan "home guard," the Boeitai (included in the above total of 155,000).[4] Intelligence informed U.S. air planners that there were some two to three thousand Japanese aircraft available in the defense of Okinawa. Despite aggressive fast-carrier suppressive strikes, that number proved remarkably accurate.[5] To counter, the United States had also greatly increased its air power. U.S. air assets available for the invasion included the fast carrier attack and escort carrier forces, U.S. and British marine aviation wings, and, importantly, Lieutenant General Harmon's Army Air Corps units.

Any analysis of the Okinawan campaign must mention the heroic activities of the picket ships surrounding Okinawa, the gun crews of the combat and combat-support vessels in the waters surrounding Okinawa, and the dedicated combat air patrol (CAP) aircraft overhead, directed by air-intercept radar squadrons. This integrated team had to attempt to intercept inbound kamikaze

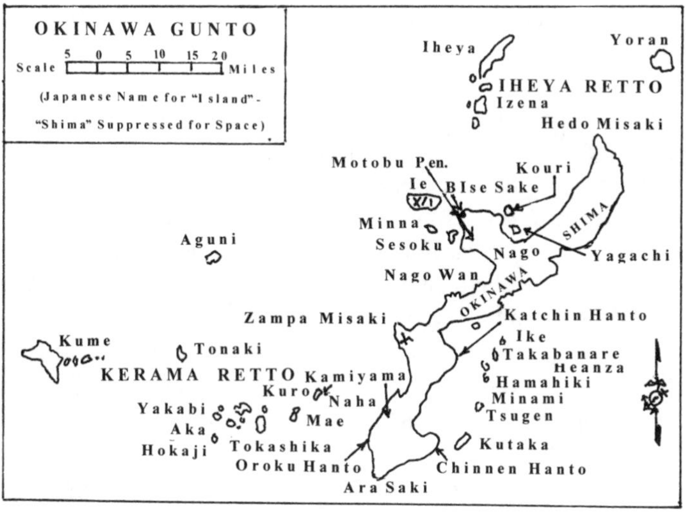
OKINAWA GUNTO
5 0 5 10 15 20
Scale Miles
(Japanese Name for "Island"-
"Shima" Suppressed for Space)
Iheya
Yoran
IHEYA RETTO
Izena
Hedo Misaki
Motobu Pen.
Kouri
Ie
Ise Sake
Minna
Sesoku
SHIMA
Aguni
Nago
Yagachi
Nago Wan
OKINAWA
Zampa Misaki
Katchin Hanto
Kume
Ike
Tonaki
Takabanare
Heanza
KERAMA RETTO
Kamiyama
Hamahiki
Kuro
Naha
Minami
Yakabi
Tsugen
Mae
Aka
Kutaka
Hokaji
Tokashika
Oroku Hanto
Chinnen Hanto
Ara Saki

Okinawa
Courtesy of the History and Museums Division, HQMC

and human-flying-bomb (baka) flights against all vessels. Around Okinawa, the kamikazes and baka bombers sank 32 Navy ships and craft and damaged 368. In the defense of Okinawa, 763 Navy aircraft were lost. The total in casualties of U.S. Navy personnel en route to and in the waters around Okinawa totaled 4,900 killed or missing in action and an additional 4,824 wounded in action.[6]

The Okinawa Campaign

Seizure of Okinawa employed six divisions, initially two Marine divisions landing on the two northern Hagushi landing beaches and two Army divisions landing on the two southern Hagushi landing beaches. In addition, two floating reserve divisions, the 2d Marine Division and the Army's 77th Infantry Division, were both landed during the campaign and took part in critical aspects of the operation. The landing force commander was Lieutenant General Buckner, whose Tenth Army staff included as Marine deputy chief of staff Brig. Gen. Oliver P. Smith.

The Northern Attack Force consisted of the III AC, under Maj. Gen Roy S. Geiger. The III AC consisted of the 1st Marine Division, under Maj. Gen. Pedro A. del Valle, and the 6th Marine

Division, under Maj. Gen. Lemuel C. Shepherd (later commandant of the Marine Corps). Upon landing, III AC swung to the north to seize the terrain north of the landing beaches to the Ishikawa Isthmus; later it would take the northern third of the island. Following defeat of all northern Japanese defenders and seizure of everything north of the Hagushi landing beaches, both Marine divisions came south, down to the Shuri Castle line, to assist the Army units whose mission was to seize the southern third of the island. The Southern Attack Force was composed of the Army's XXIV Corps under Maj. Gen. John R. Hodge. This included the 7th Infantry Division, under Maj. Gen. Archibald Arnold, and the 96th Infantry Division, under Maj. Gen. James L. Bradley. Following their landings, these units swung south and were soon embroiled in the Japanese 32d Division's main defenses centering on the Shuri Castle and farther south the capital city of Naha and its ringed defenses.[7]

The 2d Marine Division, embarked aboard amphibious shipping, complete with necessary LVTs, would, simultaneous to the actual landings on the Hagushi beaches, do a false landing off the southeastern beaches (to attempt to replicate their very successful false landing off the beaches of Tinian Town early in the Tinian operation). This feint was so realistic that the Japanese mistook the landing force as one of the major threats and diverted kamikaze flights to attack it. One LST and one attack transport took direct hits, and many casualties, by both the ships' crews and the embarked marines, were incurred.

Plans called for a pre–L-day seizure of Kerama Retto and Keise Shima (L-5 and -6), off the western coast of Okinawa, by the Army's 77th Infantry Division. This was to be preceded by recons by Maj. Jim Jones's FMFPac Amphib Recon Battalion (discussed in detail below). These were to be seized as offshore artillery bases from which Army "long toms" could fire in support of the ground assault on Okinawa proper.

All air on Okinawa was under the commander, Joint Tactical Air Force (JTAF), Maj. Gen. Francis C. Mulcahy, USMC. They were tasked to furnish land-based air support once their squadrons were ashore. This was a diverse air unit whose assets included, besides fighters from three Marine air groups (MAGs), nine fighter squadrons, two night-fighter squadrons, four air-warning squadrons (which included radar installations), an Army Air Corps fighter wing, service squadrons, an AAF photoreconnaissance squadron, two Marine torpedo-bomber squadrons, and two Marine observation squadrons (VMOs).[8]

Preparation for the landing, aside from more extensive naval gunfire on Okinawa itself (eight days), included numerous strikes by the fast-carrier attack forces under Rear Adm. Mark Mischer. These strikes were around Okinawa and the surrounding islands and on the airfields on Formosa and in southern Kyushu. British aircraft carriers participated fully in many of these prep air strikes.[9]

Intelligence for amphibious landings was, by now, fairly straightforward. Analysis of Ultra (intercepts of Japan's version of the Enigma code machine) had failed to pinpoint major details of General Ushijima's major fortifications. Japanese defensive instructions were captured, however, during the battle for Okinawa and provided further insight into the Japanese defense tactics.[10] Aerial photography did an excellent job on preparing 1:10,000 and 1:5,000 terrain maps from aerial photo interpretation.[11] The submarine *Swordfish* (Cdr. K. E. Montross) was assigned to do the periscope photography on Okinawa. It left Pearl Harbor on 22 December 1944 and was last heard from on 3 January 1945. The sub was never heard from again and was presumed lost, due to mine or other enemy action.[12]

Overview

Despite fierce opposition, both the 1st and 6th Marine Divisions made good progress toward the north of Okinawa, and by 20 April 1945, the Motobu Peninsula had been captured.

Interestingly, the use of war dogs came into its own in the battle for Motobu. Dogs, mainly German shepherds or Dobermans, would accompany assault units in heavy undergrowth and, usually, alert the marines in time to avoid an ambush. (On jungle patrols with the 17th Gurkha in Malaya against the Communist terrorists in 1959, I had the opportunity to work with patrol dogs. The Gurkha Division also had good results with these dogs. As the regimental commander of the 26th Marines in Vietnam in 1968, my regiment used many patrol dogs with great success when operating under triple-canopy jungle and in close or heavily vegetated terrain. A number of my marines were saved by the use of these dogs.)

By 1 May, the Motobu mop-up had been completed. All enemy units in northern Okinawa had either been killed or captured, with the exception of a few diehards who went to the hills. These were eventually hunted down and either captured or killed. Both the 1st and 6th Marine Divisions were now ordered south to assist the Army in the seizure of southern Okinawa. The terrain and the Japanese defenses were formidable, and units there were making slow progress and incurring a high number of casualties.

Using tanks when possible, as well as flame throwers and demolitions, the marines began to make progress. Finally, on 29 May, a company from the 1st Battalion, 5th Marines (1st Marine Division) was able to seize the heights of Shuri Castle, and the Japanese began an immediate series of very effective night tactical withdrawals. Retiring to the south, they occupied a series of redoubts, using terrain to the ultimate and continuing to whittle away the marine units. Both marine divisions continued to hammer away despite their heavy losses. Street fighting in the city of Naha was bitter. The river crossing within Naha was an opposed landing made by use of LVTs with marine engineers following on with bridging. The marines continued closing the circle at the southern end of Okinawa. In early June, a shore-to-shore beach landing on the Oruku Peninsula, preceded by all of the normal naval gunfire and air strikes, resulted in its finally being secured on 12 June.

When Lieutenant General Buckner came up to the southern front on 18 June, his command group was spotted by a Japanese artillery observer. The Japanese took the OP under fire and Buckner died within minutes of shrapnel wounds to his chest. He was the most senior U.S. military officer killed in action during World War II.

Having previously been selected for lieutenant general, Major General Geiger was immediately promoted and took over command of the Tenth Army. This was important in that this was the first time in the history of the U.S. military that a marine officer took command of an Army (composed of two amphibious corps with three divisions each). An interesting aspect of this temporary command was the fact that Geiger was a highly decorated Marine aviator occupying what would normally be considered a ground-officer's billet.

Within five days, the senior area Army lieutenant general, Joseph A. "Vinegar Joe" Stilwell, was brought in to replace Geiger. Four days prior to Stilwell's arrival (on 21 June 1945), Geiger, as Tenth Army commander, had declared Okinawa secured.[13] General Stilwell was later deputized by General MacArthur on 25 August 1945 to negotiate the "surrender" of the remaining Japanese forces in the Ryukyus.[14]

Reconnaissance Operations at Okinawa

With all of the preceding as background, the reader will have some insight into the complexity and diversity of the recon operations that were conducted. These included those on Okinawa proper, which was primarily by the respective division recon companies. The bulk of the landings on the surrounding islands were reconned and/or cleared by Maj. Jim Jones's FMFPac Amphib Recon Battalion. Okinawa reaffirmed the dictate of doubling the size of the original VAC Amphibious Reconnaissance Company, following the Tinian operation, in anticipation of a quantum increase in mission requirements (see chapter 8).

On 19 March 1945, B Company, under 1st Lt. Russ Corey, had completed its participation at Iwo Jima and returned to Saipan for R&R and refitting. Earlier in March, the remainder of the recon battalion had departed Pearl Harbor on the APDs *Scribner* (APD-123) and *Kinzer* (APD-91), en route to Leyte. They were tasked to provide pre-Okinawa amphib recon training to the Army 77th Infantry Division's Scouts in rubber-boat operations. Following a short period of instruction, and after making several practice landings with the 77th, the recon battalion (less B Company) left Leyte almost immediately for Okinawa, still aboard the APDs *Scribner* and *Kinzer.* They arrived off Kerama Retto on L-7 (25 March 1945), joining Rear Adm. I. N. Kiland's Western Islands Attack Group.[15]

Kerama Retto is a series of small, volcanic, peaklike islands lying about fifteen miles off the west coast of Okinawa in the East

China Sea. Vice Admiral Turner wanted the entire Kerama Group of islands seized prior to L day for use as a closely adjacent anchorage for vessels involved in the Okinawa operation. They would prove an ideal haven for vessels hit by kamikazes or bomb damage. Turner's plan called for both Kerama Retto and Keise Shima to be taken. Keise Shima, which consisted of three islets, was only five miles west-northwest of Naha in the East China Sea. It would serve as a "sea-based" artillery position from which the mixed Army–Marine Corps's field artillery group's 155-mm "long toms" and 155-mm guns could support the assault landings.[16]

The night of 25–26 March 1945 (L-7/L-6), A Company (Capt. Merwyn H. Silverthorn Jr.) landed by rubber boat from APDs *Scribner* (APD-122) and *Kinzer* (APD-91) and reconned the Keise Shima islets (Kuefo Shima, Naganna Shima, and Kamiyama Shima). They found them unoccupied and took them without casualties. UDTs came in offshore and cleared (blew) the coral approaches for the landing of the provisional artillery units onto these islets.[17] Elements of the Army 77th Infantry Division (3d Battalion, 306th Infantry) landed later in the day on the twenty-sixth and began taking the Kerama Retto Islands. At the same time Silverthorn's A Company was involved on Keise Shima, Corey's B Company, leaving Saipan on the *Chase* (APD-54), was en route to rejoin their parent amphib recon battalion at Kerama Retto. Following its Keise Shima recon, A Company landed on Awara Saki the night of L-5 (28 March). Awara Saki was a small island off the southern tip of Tokashiki Shima, one of the larger islands in the Kerama Retto. It also was found to be unoccupied.

The third action of FMFPac's recon battalion was the next night (L-4) by A Company on two islands: Mae Shima and Kuro Shima. When a Japanese suicide boat attempted to land on Mae Shima at 0630 hours, Captain Silverthorn's recon marines opened fire at three hundred yards with their automatic weapons and machine guns and blew the singly occupied boat out of the water.[18]

First Lieutenant Corey's B Company arrived from Saipan on L day, 1 April, off the Minatoga (east coast) beaches and joined in the feint landing of the 2d Marine Division. The recon marines did not land and fortunately did not sustain any casualties in the kamikaze attacks that struck two of their Demonstration Group Charlie's amphibious ships (the transport *Hinsdale* and LST 844).[19]

Following the main landings on L day and the Tenth Army's sweep south along the eastern coastline, Admiral Turner turned his attention to the series of eastern coastal islands off Nakagusuku Wan and Chimu Wan. Calling on Maj. Jim Jones's now-reconstituted full recon battalion, the battalion was attached to the Eastern Islands Attack and Fire Support Group. A series of landings were conducted using rubber boats from their APDs. The "guard island" for Nakagusuku Wan was the southernmost island in the group, Tsugen Shima, which lies southeast of the Katchin Peninsula. Aerial reconnaissance had picked up a number of developed Japanese positions overlooking Tsugen village. There was reportedly a 5-inch coastal defense gun there that covered the approaches to Buckner Bay. Clearly, Tsugen Shima was not going to be a walk in the moonlight.

Shortly after 0200, on the night of 5–6 April (L+4 and L+5), both A and B Companies and the Amphib Recon Battalion Headquarters, with the weapons platoon, landed on the western beaches of Tsugen Shima. Scout swimmers had gone in ahead of time and, despite the scouts finding a few civilians on the beach, signaled the remainder of their units ashore.

Just inland from the beach, the recon marines encountered four Okinawan civilians. They took two prisoners, but two escaped in the darkness and alerted the Japanese garrison. Enemy reaction was instantaneous and violent. Silverthorn's A Company began receiving heavy machine-gun fire from Tsugen village. To the north, B Company, in a like manner, was taken under immediate heavy fire from one of the Japanese trench systems (which API had located). Both units were now taking heavy mortar fire and suffering casualties. The war dogs and handlers accompanying the recon marines on this mission were all killed in the first few moments.

Major Jones, having been directed that his mission was strictly reconnaissance-to uncover Japanese defenses—determined that they had done just that. Rather than use his underweaponed, lightly equipped rubber-boat unit to engage an obviously stronger Japanese unit, Jones made the decision to withdraw.[20] Under cover of darkness, they were able to recover all of their wounded to the beach, still under heavy mortar fire. A number of their rubber boats were damaged by this mortar fire, but there were sufficient boats for the wounded and they were able to reboard the usable boats and start their return to the APDs.

Sgt. Clarence Fridley of B Company commanded five men in his recon squad: PFCs Nelson Donley, Clarence Krejci, Wiley Saucier, Donald McNees, and Phillip Dzuibek. Considered one of the best of his company, Fridley's squad was directed by First Lieutenant Corey to cover the withdrawal of the battalion from the beaches. They set up a machine gun and used their BARs and M-1 rifles. Indicative of the difficulties and problems that can be caused by local indigenous civilians in combat, as Fridley's squad was protecting their company mates carrying the wounded to the overloaded boats on the beach, a young Okinawan girl walked up in front of PFC Clarence Krejci. Not wanting to kill her, and at the same time recognizing the danger, Krejci wisely scared her away.

At nearly the same time, an elderly Okinawan gentlemen came up in front of PFC Nelson Donley. He was waving his arms and screaming. Rather than give away his position to the advancing Japanese by firing his weapon, Donley gave the old gentleman a butt stroke to the face, knocking him back and quieting the disruptive man. Had he fired, his position would have been quickly compromised. With dawn approaching, this decreasing ring of marines covering the withdrawal from the beach had to get out of there. They collectively backed down to the beach. As they approached the beach, all hands were startled to hear their machine gun firing as it was coming down to the beach with them. PFC Krejci was cradling the .30 caliber in his arms, à la John Wayne. No one kidded him about his replication of that famous scene from the World War II motion picture!

Finding no usable rubber boats, they took to the water swimming. As they reached deep water, they began dropping their weapons and swimming toward the APDs. On the way, they overtook the heavily overloaded rubber boats with their wounded aboard. They either hung on to the sides or, in the case of several who were unable to swim any farther, were hauled aboard, despite the lack of freeboard.[21]

Captain Silverthorn's A Company took two killed in action and eight wounded in action. Four days later, as a result of the enemy information developed by Major Jones's recon marines, Tsugen Shima was taken by the Army's 3d Battalion, 105th Infantry of the Army 27th Division. The island was secured by 1800 on 11 April (L+10). During the assault by the Army unit, the Japanese, true to form, opened up shortly after they hit the beaches. The Army called for naval gunfire. The cruiser *Pensacola* and several destroyers obliged, and the Army continued the attack. Tsugen Shima had been defended by approximately 300 Japanese. Of these, 234 were killed and about 50 fled but were hunted down as the island was secured several days later. Three 6-inch guns and all enemy installations were captured or destroyed. The Army unit suffered 24 killed in action and about 100 wounded.[22]

This action on Tsugen Shima was an appropriate use of recon assets, developing the enemy situation and then calling for a larger, more heavily weaponed unit supported by strong naval gunfire to "finish the job." On 11 April, 3/105 was pulled out, and, in a like manner, another Army unit came in to mop up. UDTs blew the coral and cleared the approaches for the Army landing.

The night following the recon marines' withdrawal under fire, Major Jones's recon battalion continued in its mission of clearing more offshore islands. Fifteen minutes after midnight during the early morning hours of 6 April, the entire battalion landed on Ike Shima, the northernmost of the "guard islands." There were no Japanese and only one Okinawan found on this island. Reembarking in their rubber boats, B Company then made a dawn (0530) landing on adjacent Takabanare Shima, just to the south of Ike Shima. Here Lieutenant Corey's recon marines discovered two hundred Okinawan civilians. They were frightened but generally docile. Reporting the civilians, they left them and returned to their APD.

Almost simultaneous to B Company's operations on Takabanare, two platoons of Captain Silverthorn's A Company landed by rubber boat at 0545 on Heanza Shima. Finding it unoccupied, they crossed the channel to the south and at 0800 landed on Hamahika Shima. Here they discovered fifteen hundred more civilians. These were reported, and later that day A Company reembarked aboard their APD. Later in the month, the 3/5 landed on both islands and processed these civilians. All such Okinawan civilians were eventually processed through refugee camps set up behind the III Amphibious Corps lines in the south.

On the night of 7 April, Company B landed at 2230 through heavy surf on Kutaka Shima, eight miles to the south. It was the southernmost of the "eastern islands." They found it unoccupied— no Japanese defenders, no Okinawan civilians, and no installations. Okinawan surf can be unforgiving at times. On this last landing, three rubber boats dumped in the heavy surf and one marine was drowned. At 0100 hours, the recon marines withdrew, concluding their recons of the eastern islands.[23]

The signal service performed in these eastern approach islands by the Amphib Recon Battalion, followed by the Army landings of 3/105 and the marines of 3/5, supported of course by UDT and their naval gunfire and naval shipping, opened up the eastern coast of Okinawa for use in resupply of the XXIV Corps in its drive to the south. The cross-island roads were in poor shape, causing many logistics problems. They could now be bypassed. The LSTs were then able to land directly on the eastern beaches in Nakagusuku Wan.

Encircling Okinawa, the two APDs repositioned the amphib recon battalion on the western coast of Okinawa near the Motobu Peninsula. Their mission was to assist in the Army's seizure of Ie Shima, site of a usable Japanese airfield. Located on the northwest corner of Okinawa the two islands, lying directly west of the Motobu Peninsula, Minna Shima and Ie Shima would be their next recon objectives.

Minna Shima was to be another offshore artillery fire base. The entire recon battalion made a landing on Minna Shima through moderate surf at 0445, just prior to dawn on 13 April. It took only two hours to scour the island; no Japanese defenders and only thirty Okinawan civilians were found. The recon marines then covered the potential landing beaches to protect the UDT's recon in anticipation of the Army artillery landing scheduled for 15 April. Following UDT's clearance of the approaches, the Army landed two 105-mm howitzer battalions and one 155-mm howitzer battalion. Lying just four miles south of Ie Shima, the artillery was in an excellent position to support the subsequent 77th Division landing on Ie Shima scheduled for the 305th and 306th Regiments on 16 April.

Ie Shima was taken against strong opposition by Japanese and Okinawan defenders, and by 20 April, the island was secured. The Japanese lost 4,706 killed and 149 captured. Army losses were 239 killed, 879 wounded, and 19 missing in action. The famous World War II "hometown news" war correspondent Ernie Pyle was killed by Japanese machine-gun fire while accompanying the Army 77th.[24]

Jones's recon battalion remained on Minna Shima until noon on 14 April, when they reembarked on their APDs. "Three days later," a history of the battle notes, "the battalion was released from attachment to the 77th Division and attached to III AC."[25] In mid-April, after securing many of the peripheral islands off both coasts of Okinawa, the battalion came ashore and set up a CP and bivouac site on Okinawa between missions. The marines were delighted to get off the confining spaces of their APDs, which were starting to be used as part of the picket screen for the kamikaze aircraft taking their toll on the naval picket ships in the waters surrounding Okinawa.

First Lieutenant Corey recounted one of the company's "more unusual missions" during the "on the beach phase" of the Okinawa campaign. The Ryukyu Islands are inhabited by a number of species of poisonous snakes, of which the Habu, belonging to the poisonous pit viper family, is the most deadly. Habu snakes run up to two meters in length and are dark green in color with yellow splotches. It was difficult for marines to spot them when crawling through grass. The marines in the landing force had already begun taking snakebite casualties. These occurred during their night movements and while staying low to avoid rifle and machine-gun fire, particularly around the Korean burial tombs.

For unknown reasons, the landing force medics had no antivenom to combat the poisonous Habu. When advised of the lack of antivenom, Major General Geiger asked his Corps surgeon what they could do. He was told that they could "catch Habus, milk them for their poisonous venom, and then inject the venom into horses in increasing dosages until the horses displayed immunity to the Habu bite." Then they could "extract the antivenom anti-bodies for injection into humans as the antidote for Habu snake bites."[26] Turning to his III AC Amphib Recon Battalion com-mander, Maj. Jim Jones, Geiger directed him to have his recon marines capture a quantity of Habu snakes so the Navy doctors could produce the antivenom. Corey's company ended up with the unenviable task of gathering the poisonous snakes. None of his recon marines had any experience capturing and gathering poi-sonous snakes, so, using cigarettes and C rations as barter, they persuaded the native Okinawans to gather several baskets of the deadly vipers. Apparently, the landing force soon had enough antivenom to solve the problem.

The FMFPac Amphib Recon Battalion did the bulk of the offshore island recons, switching from coast to coast off Buckner Bay and in the East China Sea as needs dictated. The organic re-con companies of the 1st and 6th Marine Divisions were, in the meantime, more active on the mainland of Okinawa.

Division Recon Companies Operations

On L day (1 April 1945), the 6th Marine Division, landing on the left (north), over Hagushi Red and Green Beaches, quickly moved inland, seizing Yontan airfield. The 22d Marines were on the left and the 29th on the right (south).

Former Raider company commander (then) Maj. Anthony "Cold Steel" Walker had taken command of the recon company of the 6th Division. Maj. Gen. Lem Shepherd sent the 140-marine company up the western coastal road of the Zampa Misaki Cape mounted on tanks. By day's end they had moved out one thou-sand yards up this cape. The next morning (L+1), the 22d Marines, using the information developed by the recon company, continued moving north to seize the remainder of the cape. During this same day, Walker's recon company, again mounted on tanks, pushed north from Kurawa across the neck of the cape and took the small town of Nagahama, effectively cutting off the base of the Zampa Misaki Peninsula.

In my interviews with Tony Walker, he confirmed the close relationship between the recon company and Shepherd: "General Shepherd used our division recon company as his eyes and ears."

Throughout the Okinawa campaign, Shepherd always gave the usually lightly weaponed recon company additional firepower and transport. Walker frequently put his troops mounted on tanks, and as a consequence, they were able to move swiftly ahead of the division line units, uncovering major Japanese defensive positions. When they were hit by obviously superior Japanese forces, they would pull back and Shepherd would send in his infantry regiments, supported by artillery, air, and naval gunfire, to overwhelm the Japanese. This proved to be a particularly effective tactic for the situation and assisted measurably in the rapid seizure of the northern third of Okinawa.[27]

By 3 April (L+2), the 6th Division had crossed the isthmus backbone along the Nagahama-Ishikawa line, sealing off all Japanese north of this line. While Major Walker's 6th Recon Company was involved in this area, to the south, Maj. Gen. Pedro del Valle's 1st Marine Division Recon Company under 1st Lt. Robert J. Powell was equally active.

On the same day, Lt. Powell's 1st Company began scouting the front of the 1st Marine Division's zone of action. Traveling along the division boundary with the 6th Marine Division to their north, they traversed by motorized patrols to the eastern shore of Okinawa at the base of Katchin Peninsula. At about 1300, having reported getting to the base of Katchin, they then were ordered to swing north up the east coast, reaching Hiazaonna, meeting only a lightly held tank trap. They were then directed to return to the 1st Marine Division lines before dark, which they did, again meeting no resistance. Col. Edward Snedeker's 7th Marines quickly followed up on the recon company's report of little enemy activity and pushed across the island to the town of Hizaonna, reaching it at 1830 on the evening of 3 April.[28] In the next few days, the 6th Marine Division continued its sweep north, reaching the port town of Nago on the west coast. UDTs and minesweepers were called in, sweeping the port and opening it for seaborne delivery of logistic support. On 6 April, the recon company was assigned a sector to mop up bypassed Japanese troops in the area between the Ishikawa Isthmus line and the Yakada-Yaka line.[29]

The upper one-third of Okinawa contains the Motobu Peninsula, a ten-by-eight-mile appendage on its west coast. The peninsula is as large as the entire island of Saipan. Firmly astride the 6th Marine Division zone of action, it had to be secured for the continued advance of III Amphibious Corp's march to secure northern Okinawa. The Japanese had withdrawn the bulk of their forces in central Okinawa, retiring to the mountainous center of the peninsula. This twelve-hundred-foot hill was called Yae-Take and would prove a formidable redoubt. Elements of the Japanese 44th Independent Brigade included two infantry battalions, an anti-tank company, and a regimental gun company. These totaled some two thousand troops defending Motobu. They had fortified Yae-Take with 75-mm artillery and 150-mm guns and 6.1-inch naval guns that had been salvaged from sunken or air-damaged Japanese ships.[30]

Major General Shepherd turned again to Major Walker's division recon company to scout ahead of his regiments. Patrolling up the west coast road out of Nago, Walker's recon troopers again were tank-mounted for increased speed and mobility. They moved ahead of the 29th Marines, reaching the coastal town of Awa. Finding only scattered resistance, the recon returned to Nago and then, in order to "fix" the enemy, swung north across the base of the Motobu Peninsula to the town of Nakasoni. On this recon, the company ran into considerably more Japanese resistance. Both going and coming, their patrol experienced a series of sharp firefights. On 9 April 1945, 2/29 used the recon company's route to Nakasoni and Unten on the northeast side of Motobu Peninsula. By the tenth they were set up in both towns.

Returning to the west coast of Motobu, Walker's recon company continued patrolling ahead of the 29th Marines up the western coast. As the Japanese had fled, they had blown many of the bridges along the coastal road. This slowed the recon company until division engineers came and either rebuilt the bridges or were able to make bypasses. By 11 April, while in the town of Toguchi, they were ordered to punch all the way up the coastal road to the tip of Motobu. They were tasked to secure the town of Bise for eventual emplacement of a radar-warning station for early warning of incoming kamikazes. Recon's secondary mission was to guard against possible Japanese reinforcement landings from seaward. They were able to secure Bise by the twelfth. Taking advantage of recon's dash, the recon marines were reinforced that evening by Fox Company from the 29th Marines. Major Walker assumed command and responsibility for the Bise area.[31]

Major Jones's amphib recon battalion was attached at this time to the 6th Marine Division to assist in the seizure of Motobu Peninsula. Their mission was the recon and seizure of three small islands lying off the Motobu coast which were believed occupied by Japanese or Okinawan Boeitai (an organization similar to the National Guard). Landing by rubber boat on the night of 19–20 April, they secured both of the two larger of the islands, Sesoko Shima off the west coast and Yagachi Shima to the north. Yagachi Shima was one of the "guard" islands for the Japanese midget-submarine base at Unten. Finding no Japanese troops, Jones's battalion was ordered to take over defense of the two islands. Kouri Shima was taken by Major Walker's 6th Marine Division Recon Company the next day. In their daylight landing, they used LVTs for both transport and their LVT(A)s provided fire support.[32]

The remainder of the 6th Division was wrapping up its reduction of Yae Take, and by 20 April, Motobu Peninsula had been declared secure. The other regiment of the 6th, the 29th Marines, had been moving north, simultaneous to the reduction of Motobu Peninsula, and by L+12 had secured all of northern Okinawa. The commandant of the Marine Corps, General Vandegrift, came out to Okinawa and on 22 April participated in the ceremony signaling of the conquest of northern Okinawa.[33]

After northern Okinawa was secured, the III AC's 1st and 6th Marine Divisions moved south to join the XXIV Corps's attack south in the Shuri Castle area. The 1st Division completed relief of the 27th Division on the lines on 1 May. The 6th Division moved into the lines on the west coast, moving southward toward the capitol city of Naha. Heavy spring rains had turned Okinawa's roads into quagmires, slowing the attacks southward.

When both marine divisions were released from their actions to the north, marine leaders could foresee the meat-grinding casualties that the Army was taking. They strongly recommended that the III AC's amphibious assets be used in an "end-run" amphibious assault on the southern end of the islands. After consideration, Lieutenant General Buckner declined and opted instead to put both Marine divisions into the lines. In retrospect, most Marine commanders found this to be a failure to properly use this valuable asset and contend that many casualties could have been avoided had permission been granted.[34]

By 12 May, the 22d Marines had been able to seize the heights above the northern reaches of the city of Naha. The Japanese did not share General Buckner's apparent aversion to use of amphibious forces; on the night of 14–15 May, they attempted counterlandings off the west coast. These were broken up and destroyed by Navy patrol craft and other vessels in the area. General Shepherd reinforced the 22d Marines along the coast with Major Walker's recon company, and no further threat from the sea materialized.[35]

On 25 May 1945, the 6th Division elements were in the outskirts of Naha city. There was a twenty-yard-wide canal that connected Kokuba Estuary and the Asato River to the west and effectively divided the city, constituting a significant obstacle. The bottom was laden with mud, and there were three- to five-foot stone banks. The 6th Recon Company crossed the Asato River and took over the western part of Naha. Opposed by snipers, these were quickly taken out by Walker's recon marines. With this foothold, marine engineers rapidly completed a footbridge across the mouth of the Asato River. Although there were a number of counterattacks during the night, these were broken up by artillery and the marines in the line. Pressure continued on the drive south, with the 29th Marines coming into the line to relieve the 4th Marines. The 22d Marines then moved into the western portions of the city of Naha. In order to withdraw the 22d Marines for action elsewhere on the line, General Shepherd shortly thereafter had his division recon company on 29 May take over this western part of Naha. In this relief, his G-3, Lt. Col. Victor H. Krulak, whimsically made Major Walker "the mayor of western Naha." With bridging, the recently withdrawn 22d Marines made an opposed river crossing on the 29th of May, crossing Kokuba estuary and establishing a riverhead on the eastern shore.[36]

In order to complete the seizure of Naha and its airfield, Shepherd requested approval from III AC and the Tenth Army to seize the Oruku Peninsula by amphibious assault, shore to shore.

Receiving approval from on high, he sent Walker's recon scouts by rubber boats onto the Oruku Peninsula. Crossing during the night of 1 June, four small groups of scouts infiltrated the northern portions of the Oruku. Although they were taken under fire, they were able to listen and observe the enemy activity on Oruku. Reporting on their return, they advised that the peninsula was defended but that "the enemy was not there in great strength." Importantly, they determined that the beaches were usable by LVTs. Following up on these recon reports, the 4th Marines boarded their LVTs near Machinato airfield on 5 June and made a successful amphibious landing on the north flank of the Japanese defenders and secured a beachhead on Oruku for further reduction of its Japanese defenders.[37]

Simultaneous to the 4th Marines landing on Oruku, following a brief but intensive firefight, Major Walker's 6th Recon Company seized Ona Yama Island in the middle of Naha Harbor.[38] It took ten days of hard fighting by the 1st Marine Division to complete the seizure of Oruku Peninsula and the elimination of Rear Adm. Minoru Ota and his Rikusentai force.[39]

East of the Naha and Oruku Peninsula operations, Maj. Gen. Pedro del Valle's 1st Marine Division Recon Company under First Lieutenant Powell, was spearheading the attacks of Col. Edward Snedeker's 7th Marine Regiment. On 3 June 1945, the recon unit uncovered the approaches to Kokuba, and the 7th Marines quickly seized this, one of the last major objectives in its sweep to the south.[40]

Amphib Recon Battalion Takes the Western Offshore Islands

Concomitant to the 1st and 6th Marine Division's final recon operations on the southern tip of Okinawa, FMFPac's amphib recon battalion had several final missions in the East China Sea, on the islands off the west coast. The first of these was the recon of Kumi Shima to the west.

On the night of 13–14 June, B Company, under 1st Lt. Russell Corey, conducted a recon of Kumi Shima. Finding mostly Okinawan civilians there, they withdrew. Major Jones's entire amphib recon battalion landed on the island later, on 26 June, from LST 1040. For this landing and seizure, the recon battalion was reinforced by A Company, 1/7. They took over occupation of this offshore island. The diary of B Company's PFC Nelson Donley reveals that they encountered a "large number of civilians. The Japanese had a radio relay station operated by some 25–30 soldiers."[41]

This seizure of Kumi Shima was not only to complete continued seizure of offshore islands but, more important, to obtain another offshore site for a U.S. early warning radar site for continuing kamikaze attacks. The amphib recon, reinforced with A Company, 1st Battalion, 7th Marines, remained on Kumi Shima until 27 July, when they were relieved by Army units. The recon battalion departed for Okinawa aboard the *Elkhart* (APA-80) and remained aboard, lying offshore of Okinawa. After 6 August, when news of the dropping of the atomic bomb was announced, they were diverted to Ulithi, arriving on the eleventh. With the second atomic bomb and the subsequent Japanese capitulation, the *Elkhart* was ordered to return to Okinawa. The war over, Major Jones and his recon marines cast about for a quicker "ride home." They were able to secure space for return to Pearl Harbor on the transport *President Johnson* and departed 26 August. This signaled the end of their World War II reconnaissance activities.[42]

Division Recon Company Takes the Eastern Offshore Islands

At the same time B Company of the FMFPac Amphib Recon Battalion was carrying out the recon of Kumi Shima, off the western coast of Okinawa, Maj. Tony Walker's 6th Marine Division Recon Company was ordered by General Shepherd to seize Senaga Shima, a small rocky island some one thousand yards off the southern and western coast of Oruku Peninsula. They had scouted it three days earlier. Augmented with a rifle company from 1/9, Walker's reinforced recon company landed using LVT(A)s and secured the island without resistance. The intensive four days of pre-landing prep fires had done the job, and Walker found nothing but dead Japanese and destruction of all major facilities. This appears to be the last major recon activity of Walker's recon company in the war.[43]

The 8th Marines of the 2d Marine Division had been sent back to Saipan on 11 April, after its participation in the feint landings on L day on 1 April. They were again alerted for participation in the capture of the western islands of Aguni and Iheya. In conjunction with total seizure of these western islands, a special landing force of a reinforced rifle company from the 165th Infantry made an unopposed landing on Tori Shima on 12 May, and a Marine detachment for Marine Air Warning Squadron 1 landed and began immediate operation.[44]

On 2 June, the Offshore Island Attack Force, commanded by Rear Admiral Reifsnider, with the ADC of the 2d Marine Division, Brig. Gen. Leroy P. Hunt as landing force commander, steamed from the Hagushi transport area to seize Aguni Shima and Iheya Jima. Following pre-landing bombardment and air strikes, the 8th Marines landed on Iheya Jima on 3 June, securing it. Their only casualties were from friendly fire "shorts" from the prep rocket and naval gunfire. When the 2d Marine Division Recon Company scouted Iheya Jima, they reported observing no enemy troops. No enemy defenses or Japanese defenders were found. There were, however, some three thousand Okinawan civilians located who were quickly processed by military government civil affairs teams.[45]

Using organic 2d Marine Division Reconnaissance Company scouts, on the night of 23 June, the next larger island to the south, Izena Jima, was reconned and found to be without Japanese defenders. They did locate four thousand Okinawans, but they were described as "friendly to Americans."[46]

Despite diligent research, the reconnaissance patrols in the western offshore islands of Okinawa in June and July 1945 appear to be the last recorded combat amphibious reconnaissance operations during World War II. Although not formally documented in any of the usual historical treatises, it is more probable than not that recon elements of the 1st, 2d, and 6th continued to participate in mopping-up operations on Okinawa after it had been declared secure until shortly before they departed the island.

Conclusion

Following its last actions on Okinawa, Maj. Jim Jones's FMFPac Amphib Recon Battalion returned to Pearl Harbor via Ulithi and Eniwetok anchorages, arriving in Pearl 12 September. Five days later, the battalion was disbanded and the bulk of its troops were sent to the replacement battalion at Pearl Harbor. The vast majority had sufficient "points" (which determined eligibility for discharge) and left for the United States aboard LST 761.[1]

After Okinawa was declared secure, the 1st Marine Division remained on Okinawa and set up rehabilitation camps on Motobu Peninsula. The 2d Marine Division's 8th Marine Regiment and the attached division recon company departed Okinawa and were back with their parent units on Guam by 12 July. The 6th Marine Division moved out to Guam between 4 and 11 July.[2]

The Japanese formally surrendered on 10 August 1945. The first atomic bomb was dropped on 6 August on Hiroshima, and the second followed on 9 August, hitting Nagasaki. These prompted the Japanese to agree to the terms set forth in the Potsdam Declaration.[3]

Occupation of Japan, Korea, and China

Planning had been under way for the eventual invasion of Japan. Following Japan's acceptance of the Potsdam Declaration, Pacific commanders selected the forces and method of entry to implement early occupation of the homeland islands. The surrender ceremony was scheduled aboard the battleship *Missouri* in Tokyo Bay on 2 September 1945.[4]

The Marine III Amphibious Corps, then headquartered on Guam, turned to China, its 6th Marine Division landing at

Tsingtao on the Shantung Peninsula on the east China coast. Some ten days later, on 30 September, the 1st Marine Division landed at Tientsin in northern China.[5] Both of these divisions began accepting surrender, demobilization, and return of Japanese troop units to homeland Japan.

Thus, after the close of fighting (other than mopping-up, which continued for some time), the six marine divisions were disposed of during September and October 1945 as follows: the 1st Marine Division was sent to northern China; the 2d Marine Division was sent to Kyushu in Japan; following Iwo, the 3d Marine Division had returned to Guam while the 4th Marine Division returned to Maui; the 5th Marine Division joined the 2d Marine Division in occupying Kyushu Island in Japan; and the 6th Marine Division landed on the Shantung Peninsula on the central China coast.[6]

Postwar downsizing continued throughout the Marine Corps. In China, by April 1946, the 6th Marine Division had been redesignated as the Third Marine Brigade and reduced to a reinforced regiment.[7] The 4th Marine Division on Maui returned to Camp Pendleton (where it had been initially formed) and was disestablished on 3 November 1945. In like manner, the 3d Marine Division—"less 1/3 in the Bonins and 2/21 on Truk—was disbanded on Guam." On 28 December,[8] the 5th Marine Division departed Sasebo from its occupation duty back to Camp Pendleton, where it was disestablished on 5 February the following year.[9]

By the spring of 1946, the Corps was further reduced to two small divisions, the 1st to be at Camp Pendleton, California, and the 2d to be at Camp Lejeune, North Carolina.[10] Marine air wings (MAWs) and groups went through similar downsizing and disestablishment, resulting in just two MAWs, the 2d MAW at Cherry Point and the 1st MAW at El Toro, for air support of the 1st and 2d Marine Divisions.[11] The full wartime strength of the Marine Corps was thus reduced from 485,837 to 92,222 by the end of June 1947.[12]

Rancorous debate by primarily Army-backed critics tried vainly to eliminate the Marine Corps as being a redundancy to the Army, which had proven it too could conduct amphibious operations. This assault on the Corps's very existence was ably squelched and, in 1947, the National Security Act of 1947 was enacted into law. It clarified the function of the Marine Corps and set its minimum strength at three divisions and three air wings. In 1957 legislation made the commandant of the Marine Corps a full member of the Joint Chiefs of Staff.[13]

Reconnaissance Between the End of World War II and Korea

Each of the two marine divisions, in between wars, was downsized but did include a reduced-size "division reconnaissance company." Following disestablishment of FMFPac's amphibious reconnaissance battalion in September 1945, for a time there were no force-level recon units left in the Corps.

These downsized recon units continued their specialized training in scouting and patrolling and rubber boat/submarine training. New developments in underwater swimming, including the introduction of SCUBA (self-contained underwater breathing apparatus) in the early 1950s and, later, oxygen rebreathers, wet suits, and so on, began to be included in the division recon companies T/Os and T/Es.

When the Korean War broke out in June 1950, first deployed was the 1st Marine Brigade, followed by the entire 1st Marine Division, which sailed to the sound of guns. The 1st Marine Division Recon Company was under the inspiring leadership of Capt. (later Maj. Gen.) Kenneth J. Houghton. The recon company's exploits included many critical land recon missions during the early days of the Pusan Perimeter. Following the Inchon landing in September 1950, they made a night recon and crossing of the Han River under fire. During fluid battles in 1951, they performed yeoman service in covering the flanks of the division. Its outstanding performance in Korea ensured it a continuing place for recon in the fabric of the Marine Corps.[14]

After some two years of the Korean War, the generals at both FMFLANT and FMFPac recommended to the then-commandant, Gen. Clifton B. Cates, that the Corps must revisit the corps-level reconnaissance capability. Corps commanders needed their own "eyes and ears" and should not rely on the already heavily tasked division reconnaissance companies. Maj. Regan Fuller formed the first of these post–World War II force-level recon units in his 2d Amphib Recon Battalion in 1950 at Camp Lejeune. On the west coast at Camp Pendleton, a force-level amphibious reconnaissance company, FMFPac was reestablished as a "cadre" for possible future expansion into a similar force-level recon battalion.[15] With the reformation of the 3d Marine Division, which had previously been authorized by the 1947 National Security Act, the Corps now had three division recon companies and two small force-level recon units.

From 1952 to 1955, I was privileged to head the Amphibious Reconnaissance School of Troop Training Unit Pacific (TTU PAC) at the Naval Amphibious Base in Coronado, California. Concerned about the lack of development in more sophisticated techniques for the emplacement of recon personnel deep behind the lines, I went to CG TTU PAC, Brig. Gen. Lewis B. "Chesty" Puller, with recommendations on parachuting and new methods of submarine entry for amphibious and deeper reconnaissance. Convinced that this needed to be pursued, Chesty wrote the CMC, outlining these proposals. General Shepherd agreed and sent me for a year with the Army at Fort Benning for, among other things, parachute training. Upon completion, I was ordered to the newly formed Marine Corps Test Unit One (MCTU#1) at Camp Pendleton. Among many tasks this experimental unit was given was the evaluation of the nuclear-age Marine Corps. This was for the development of the tactics, techniques, and organization for deep reconnaissance for the battlefield of the future.

I was assigned as the reconnaissance/pathfinder project officer at MCTU#1. For three years, we operated and trained at Camp Pendleton and the Naval Parachute Test Facility at NAAS El Centro. Operations were conducted at many other locations on the West Coast, operating with helicopters from the 1st Marine Air Wing and with the fleet (submarines, surface, and naval aviation forces). This time was spent working with Lt. Col. Regan Fuller and Capt. Joseph Z. Taylor in developing new tactics and techniques for the age of helicopter assault to support deep reconnaissance for the Marine Corps. This included developing new techniques of entry, such as parachute entry by recon and pathfinder teams from carriers at sea and enhancing submarine entry. The latter involved developing operational methods of submerged entry by buoyant ascents and locking back in to submerged submarines. One of the new missions added within the Marine Corps was the development, equipping, and training of pathfinder teams for insertion prior to marine helicopter landings for guidance and control of such assaults. This period of development at Test Unit One from 1954 to 1957 is described in my book *Fortune Favors the Brave*.[16]

This led to the formation of the first of the Corps's force reconnaissance companies, the only FMF unit to be established upon the conclusion of Test Unit One's lengthy mission of development. I was privileged to be assigned, as a major, to become the first commanding officer of this new force-level reconnaissance unit. 1st Force Recon Company was established on 19 June 1957 with a strength of 14 officers and 147 enlisted marines and corpsmen; a company headquarters with an exec; an S-3 operations officer; a communications section with a comm officer; and initially three specialized platoons. At the beginning there was one amphibious reconnaissance platoon (trained primarily in submarine/swimming/rubber boat entry) broken down into five four-man amphib recon teams, a parachute reconnaissance platoon with similar five four-man teams, and a parachute pathfinder platoon with three parachute pathfinder teams of 1 officer and 10 enlisted each. During our first year in the Fleet Marine Force, it became apparent that we could cross-train the divers and parachutists. After the first year, the company exec, Capt. Joseph Z. Taylor, took half of our jumpers and divers and formed 2d Force Recon at Camp Lejeune. Capt. Paul X. Kelley became his exec (Kelley later became commandant).[17]

In the acid test of FMF capability, the entire company deployed to the Philippines (Luzon) for participation in the largest simultaneous helicopter landing in Marine Corps history, Operation Strongback. The Marine Expeditionary Force commander was Maj. Gen. David M. Shoup, soon to be commandant of the Marine Corps. This operation solidified the continuing requirement for force-level recon in the Marine Corps.[18]

During Vietnam, four additional force recon companies were formed (the 3d, 4th, 5th, and 6th), four of which served in Vietnam. 1st Force can look with pride to its role in the first combat parachute jumps in Marine Corps history. The Paramarines, formed in 1942 and disbanded in 1944, always served in ground-combat roles and never made a combat jump. The first force recon jump was some thirty-five miles behind enemy lines near Chu Lai.[19]

Both force recon companies and the two division recon battalions performed superbly in Vietnam. One recon marine in our recon community, Gy. Sgt. Jimmy Howard, was awarded the Medal of Honor, scores received Navy Crosses, and many were awarded Silver and Bronze Stars. A high proportion of both the force and division recon marines were awarded the Purple Heart.

Typical deep inserts of force recon marines placed them from ten to twenty miles behind enemy lines. The bulk of these inserts and recoveries were made by helicopter, usually at either dusk or dawn. These patrols were generally composed of six marines, all heavily armed, their duration typically ran from two to four days. For detailed descriptions of many of these deep inserts, the reader is encouraged to see Lt. Cdr. Stubbe and Michael L. Lanning's *Inside Force Recon*. Other books covering force recon's Vietnam activities include Lt. Col. Alex Lee's *Force Recon Command*, and Maj. Bruce H. "Doc" Norton's *Force Recon Diary, 1969*, which chronicles a patrol member's experiences.

Following Vietnam, there was a draw-down of recon units, much as happened after World War II. At one point force reconnaissance was virtually disestablished, with only a handful of force recon marines placed in a "deep recon platoon" within the division recon battalions. In a yo-yo-like manner, force recon companies would initially stand independently, then, because of complaints of overcommitment, be placed as "just another company" within division's recon battalion. Numerous studies and strong recommendations from former force recon officers concluded that placement of the force-level recon company as "just another recon company" was a mistake.[20] When Gen. James Jones Jr. became commandant of the Marine Corps, he vowed to "fix recon." He has done that, with the recent emergence of force recon companies from within the division recon battalions structure to again permit them to "stand alone," directly under the FMFLANT and FMFPac commanders for operational control.

Reconnaissance marines now have their own military occupational specialty (MOS). The basic recon man (MOS 0321) is now followed with additional MOS qualifications as the recon marine becomes more fully trained, for example, 8652 when parachute qualified, 8653 when SCUBA/UBA (underwater breathing apparatus) trained or qualified, and 8654 when the recon marine is parachute and SCUBA/UBA qualified.[21]

In the numerous actions over the years since Vietnam, including Grenada, Haiti, Somalia, the Persian Gulf, and Kosovo, marine recon was there and did well behind enemy lines. They have operated in support of major Marine, Army, Navy (SEALs), and, in some cases, Allied forces. In the summer of 2002, the commandant of the Marine Corps, Gen. James Jones, (son of Maj. Jim Jones of World War II fame) announced that henceforth the Marine Corps would provide force recon marines to operate with Special Operations (SpecOp) Command. This relatively new element of the national command structure contains Army Special Forces (Green Berets), Navy SEALs, and Air Force Special Operations Squadrons. Now it has force recon–trained marines.

From the earliest days of the Observer Group and their predecessors coming off submarines off Puerto Rico, through the atoll recons during the early days in the Pacific, through the patrols throughout the Solomons, to recons of the larger islands and the seizures of Iwo Jima and Okinawa, amphibious recon marines and their corpsmen have been a breed apart. Criticized on occasion as being an "elite within an elite," nevertheless, recon is their assigned mission. As this book is being written, another chapter has been added to their history, this time in the sands of Iraq. Prisoner recovery, screening to the front of the 1st Marine Expeditionary Force, the taking of Baghdad and Tikrit—they have again proven their merit in the crucible of combat. God bless, and may they have continued success.

Glossary

Alamo Force (or Unit)   Code name for the U.S. Sixth Army, commanded by Lt. Gen. Walter Krueger. In order to avoid this unit from being commanded by the Australian general Sir Thomas A. Blamey, commander of all Allied Land Forces in the South Pacific, General MacArthur directed the Sixth Army to operate under the code name Alamo Force. This permitted him to employ it under his personal command as part of the South West Pacific Area.

Allied Intelligence Bureau   Sometimes Allied Intelligence Force (*see* Coastwatchers)

amphib recon   A unit or the personnel of a unit whose primary mission is to conduct amphibious reconnaissance. Also a generic term describing the conduct of a reconnaissance of a beach area by seaward means, for example, rubber boats, swimmers, or scuba divers from a parent vehicle at sea.

APD   High-speed destroyer transport. Developed at the start of World War II and used for transport of Marine recon, UDT, and small special warfare forces.

battalion   A Marine tactical unit composed of a number of companies. Named for the primary element, for example, infantry battalion. Size varies, but approximately twelve hundred marines.

BLT   Battalion landing team. A balanced reinforced Marine infantry battalion with tanks, artillery, reconnaissance, and logistic support. Contains approximately two thousand marines.

Boeitai   The equivalent of our National Guard, they were encountered in the battle for Okinawa. They were well-trained and fought tenaciously along with their Japanese Army mentors.

boondockers   Marine field shoes used in World War II and the Korean War.

CEC   Civil Engineer Corps (naval engineers)

CMC   Commandant, Marine Corps. The general officer commanding the Marine Corps, and a member of the Joint Chiefs of Staff.

CNO   Chief of naval operations. The senior officer of the Navy, and a member of the Joint Chiefs of Staff.

Coastwatchers   Personnel left behind or later inserted along coastal areas on islands. Equipped with radios and local native assistance, they provided advance information on Japanese vessel and aircraft movements. Initially, primarily Australian or New Zealand personnel, they were later augmented with marine personnel. Sometimes referred to as Allied Intelligence Bureau.

combat swimming   A term applied to the techniques of reconnaissance entry by underwater swimmers and water survival. The designation fell into disuse after World II.

Corps   A term referring to the Marine Corps (when capitalized) and the next higher unit above a Marine division, commanded usually by a lieutenant general.

CP   Command post. Location of a unit's headquarters in the field.

DE   Destroyer escort

DD   Navy destroyer

D-day   The particular day on which a military operation is to commence. A means of providing a time line for a specific operation. Measured in days, for example, D-45, D-30, and so on. For different or separate landings in a larger operation, sometimes other letters were substituted in lieu of *D*, as in, for example, W day and J day.

Exec   Slang term for the second in command of a ship, unit, battalion, squadron, company, and so on.

Fairbairn-Sykes   A stiletto-like fighting knife used by Marine recon during World War II. Initially developed by Maj. Sam Yeats of the 4th Marines in Shanghai, its further development was by Inspectors (Lt. Col.) William Fairbairn and Sykes of the Shanghai Municipal Police. It was later adopted by the Royal Marine Commandos and elements of Marine Raider and Paramarine battalions.

fale   Native hut in Micronesia made of palm log frame with palm fronds thatched for roof and sides.

fantail   The aftermost deck area topside on a ship or submarine. On a submarine, it is the weather deck aft of the conning tower. On APDs, it is the area aft of the superstructure on the main deck, used primarily for the launching of rubber boats.

FLEX   Fleet landing exercise. Large training operation involving many ships, troops, and aircraft. Used before World War II to develop amphibious tactics and doctrines.

FMFPac   Fleet Marine Force, Pacific

foredeck   A term applied to the forward section of the weather deck on a vessel. On a submarine, it is the weather deck forward of the conning tower.

G-2   Intelligence officer of a Marine division. Lower units such as regiments and battalions would be S-2.

G-3   Operations officer of a division. Also S-3.

hari-kari   Ritual suicide by disembowelment with a sword, formerly practiced by samurai when disgraced or sentenced. During World War II, marines' usage of the term grew to include other forms of self-destruction, including use of hand grenades, immolation, or use of their own weapons.

H-hour   Specific hour on D-day that a particular operation is to commence.

HQMC   Headquarters Marine Corps

hydrography   The science of determining the underwater configuration of a beach or harbor area. Important to UDT and marine recon swimmers.

JICPOA   Joint Intelligence Center, Pacific Ocean Area. Centralized intelligence center, including document translation, photo interpretation, and hydrographic intelligence (charts and maps).

kamikaze   Literally, "divine wind." Japanese suicide planes that were usually flown from airfields on Kyushu and surrounding islands. Used initially against U.S. shipping off Iwo Jima and more extensively off Okinawa.

mae-west   Inflatable life preserver. Smaller than a regular aviator or troop-type flotation device. Fits over the head, with adjustable straps around the back and arms.

Marine division   A force of four or more regiments with supporting arms and logistics support, commanded by a major general. Usually about twenty thousand marines. Generally teamed with a Marine air wing (comparable command of aircraft and aircraft support). Two or more divisions form a corps.

NCDU   Naval combat demolition units. These units were jointly manned by Navy, Marine, and Army demolition specialists. Predecessor to Navy UDT.

OP   Observation post

Paramarines   Elite parachute units of battalion size that were organized during World War II. Fought with distinction as infantry units in South Pacific. Disestablished in 1944.

PBY   The Lockheed Catalina, a twin-engine amphibious flying boat. Used in World War II for patrol and limited attack and, on occasion, for surface drop and pickup of reconnaissance personnel.

periscope photography   Photographs taken through the periscope of a submerged submarine. Usually taken to supplement aerial photography. Usually show major terrain features, beach defensive installations, and the beaches of an objective area.

pidgin   A simplified language containing the vocabulary of two or more languages, used for rudimentary communications between peoples not having a common language. Used here to describe the communication between English speakers and natives of the southern and western Pacific, particularly the Solomon Islands.

PT   Patrol torpedo boats (sometimes called motor torpedo boats). Used in the Solomon Islands, Treasury Islands, Rabaul, and so on to drop and recover marine recon teams.

RAN   Royal Australian Navy. Also RANVR (Royal Australian Navy Volunteer Reserve).

rifle company   A Marine tactical infantry unit composed of a number of rifle platoons and a small headquarters.

Rikusentai   Japanese special landing force (somewhat equivalent to U.S. Marines)

rubber boats   A generic term applied to inflatable boats of varying sizes. Specified as LCR(L), landing craft rubber, large (ten-man); LCR(M) (seven-man); and LCR(S) (three-man).

SEALs   A special elite U.S. Navy warfare unit capable of overt action in littoral areas and formed from UDT units. Stands for *sea-air-l*and.

Special Forces   Elite U.S. Army unit trained in antiguerrilla operations, popularly known as the Green Berets. Marine Force Recon trains and operates with Special Forces.

surf zone   The term used in hydrography and amphib recon to designate the area of breaking surf, from the water line to the outermost line of breakers.

SWPA   South West Pacific Area. Acronym given to General Douglas MacArthur's forces, headquartered in Australia.

T/E   Table of equipment. The list of all major items of equipment—weapons, radios, and so forth—authorized for a particular Marine unit.

T/O   Table of organization. The list of all personnel authorized for a particular unit in carrying out its standard mission.

UDT   Underwater demolition team. Specially trained for the conduct of inshore hydrographic reconnaissance and for demolition of beach obstacles. Until 1944 was manned by Navy, Army, and Marine demolitionists; later became an all-Navy unit.

USA   United States Army

USAAF   United States Army Air Forces (in 1946 became the USAF, the United States Air Force)

USMC   United States Marine Corps

USMCR   United States Marine Corps Reserve

USN   United States Navy

USNR   United States Naval Reserve

utilities   Marine dungarees or field utility uniform

White Beach, Yellow Beach, etc.   Color-designated landing sites for amphibious options (e.g., White Beach 1, White Beach 2, Yellow Beach 1)

Notes

Chapter 1. In the Beginning

1. Gen. Holland M. Smith, "The Development of Amphibious Tactics in the U.S. Navy," *Marine Corps Gazette* 30, no. 9 (September 1946): 43–47.
2. Gen. Holland M. Smith and Percy Finch, *Coral and Brass* (New York: Scribner's, 1949), 84.
3. W. H. McKelvy Jr., CO Company F, 2d Battalion 5th Marines, "Report of Operations during Puerto Rico Campaign, 2–3Mar38," 4 February 1938, and enclosure I, "Attack Force Order of 2Feb38," to Commander U.S. Fleet Training Detachment, USS *New York.*
4. See Jon T. Hoffman, *Once a Legend: "Red Mike" Edson of the Marine Raiders* (Novato, Calif.: Presidio Press, 1994), 131; Bruce F. Meyers, *Fortune Favors the Brave* (Annapolis: Naval Institute Press, 2000), 88.
5. See Chief of Naval Operations, *Landing Operations Doctrine,* sec. 6, "Reconnaissance Patrols."

Chapter 2. The Units

1. Leo Shinn, "Amphibious Reconnaissance," *Marine Corps Gazette* 29, no. 4 (April 1945): 50–51; Gordon Rottman, *U.S. Marine Corps 1941–45,* Military Book Club edition (London: Osprey, 1998), 26; and *Amphibious Operation's Intelligence,* pamphlet (Quantico, Va.: Amphibious Patrols, 1948), sec. 4, p. 24.
2. Capt. Charles E. Patrick, original member of Observer Group, interview with author, Force Reconnaissance Association Reunion, Dallas, Texas, 6 June 1987.
3. Brig. Gen. Russell E. Corey, telephone interviews with author, 17 July 2002 and 17 May 2003, and Corey to author, 15 June 2002, copy of orders to Submarine School from General Corey in author's papers; also Patrick interview, 3 June 2002.
4. Corey telephone interviews.
5. Gordon Rottman, *U.S. Marine Corps, 1941–45.* (London: Osprey, 1998), 27.
6. Benis M. Frank, Marine Corps historian, quoted in Charles D. Melson and Paul Hanon's *Marine Recon, 1940–1990* (London: Osprey, 1998).
7. Frank and Shaw, *History* 3:185.
8. Charles D. Melson, "Recon Marines: Amphibious and Ground Reconnaissance Units," unpublished monograph, Historical Division, HQMC, n.d., 5; Larry Q. Zedric, *Silent Warriors of World War II: The Alamo Scouts Behind Japanese Lines* (Ventura, Calif.:

Pathfinder, 1995), 38; Susan L. Marquis, *Unconventional Warfare: Rebuilding U.S. Special Operations Forces* (Washington, D.C.: Brookings Institution, 1997), 20–23.

9. See Ralph Chester Williams, "Amphibious Scouts and Raiders," *Military Affairs* 13, no. 3 (1949): 150–57; Morison, *History* 8:166.

10. See previously secret report, CinC, United States Fleet, Headquarters of Commander in Chief, COMINCH P-997, "Invasion of the Marianas, June to August 1944," n.d.

11. Commander, Fifth Amphibious Force to CinCPac, report, "Underwater Demolition Teams, Recommendations Concerning-Based on Experience in Flintlock" (Kwajalein), 2 June 1944, declassified from secret.

12. Meyers, *Fortune Favors the Brave,* 3–8.

13. Morison, *History* 7:37–51.

14. See Morison, *History* 5:11; J. L. Zimmerman, "Island Coastwatchers," *Marine Corps Gazette* 30, no. 1 (January 1946): 16–18; Rafael Steinberg, *Island Fighting, World War II,* collector's edition (New York: Time–Life Books, 1978), 38; Williams, "Amphibious Scouts and Raiders," 150–51.

15. Edward N. Rydalch, CO Marine Corps Test Unit One, to Randolph McCall Pate, CMC, report, "Amphibious Reconnaissance, Parachute Reconnaissance and Parachute Pathfinder Matters, Recommendations Concerning," 28 March 1957, copy in History and Museums Division, HQMC; enclosure (1), 1–3: "Concept of Employment: c. (1) Amphibious reconnaissance of at least nine (9) BLT landing beaches, during the pre–D-Day period. Provision of the same number of coast-watcher stations or inland observation posts after D-Day." MCTU#1 Files, Historical Division, HQMC, Washington, D.C., copy in author's files.

Chapter 3. Tools of the Trade

1. Headquarters V Amphibious Corps, "Reconnaissance Patrols Landing on Hostile Shores," Corps Training Memorandum No. 25–44, 25 March 1944, 62A-2086, Box 20 "Reconnaissance," World War II, History and Museums Division, HQMC, Washington, D.C. Formerly confidential, now declassified.

2. Ibid.

3. Data on all submarines and other ships described come from Chief of Naval Operations, *Dictionary of American Fighting Ships,* 7 vols. (Washington, D.C.: GPO, 1968).

4. Hoffman, *Once a Legend,* 131; and Meyers, *Fortune Favors the Brave,* 3–8.

5. Col. William F. Coleman, "Amphibious Recon Patrols," *Marine Corps Gazette* 29, no. 12 (December 1945): 22–23, and vol. 30, no. 1 (January 1946): 13–15; also Meyers, *Fortune Favors the Brave,* 1–3; on Alamo Scouts usage, see Zedric, *Silent Warriors,* 1–18.

6. Morison, *History* 2:262–63; Coleman, "Amphibious Recon Patrols," 21–25; Sgt. Frank X. Tolbert, "The Advance Man," *Leatherneck* 2, no. 5 (March 1945): 3–5.

7. Smith and Finch, *Coral and Brass,* 99; Company B, Amphib Recon Battalion, FMF did waterborne recons of Kama Rock and Kangoku Rock off the northwestern coast of Iwo Jima on 12 March 1945, using twelve Amtracs. Nelson Donley Papers, copies in author's files.

8. James Logan Jones Sr., "Report of Readiness, Amphibious Reconnaissance Battalion Corps Troops, V Amphibious Corps," 30 June 1944, Annex D: Weapons; Marine Corps Table of Organization E-333, Amphibious Reconnaissance Company, Amphibious Reconnaissance Battalion, approved 28 April 1944, copy at History and Museums Division, HQMC. With respect to weapons, see Melson and Hanon, *Marine Recon, 1940–1990,* 6–7.

9. Robert A. Buerlein, *Allied Military Fighting Knives and the Men Who Made Them Famous* (Richmond, Va.: American Historical Foundation, 1984), 73–90.

10. Headquarters V Amphibious Corps, "Reconnaissance Patrols Landing on Hostile Shores," 7–8.

11. Carl Hoffman, *The Seizure of Tinian,* historical monograph (Washington, D.C.: Historical Division, HQMC, 1951), 22–23.

12. Morison, *History* 7:181.

Chapter 4. Training

1. Amphibious Corps, Pacific Fleet, Camp Elliot, San Diego, California, *Reconnaissance Patrols Landing on Hostile Shores,* Corps Intelligence Order No. 4–42, 29 October 1942, 62A–2086, Box 20, "Reconnaissance," 2–3, World War II, History and Museums Division, HQMC.

2. Headquarters V Amphibious Corps, "Reconnaissance Patrols Landing on Hostile Shores," 3.

3. See Merrill L. Bartlett and Dirk A. Ballendorf, *Pete Ellis: An Amphibious Warfare Prophet* (Annapolis: Naval Institute Press, 1996).

4. Zedric, *Silent Warriors,* 43–93; see Meyers, *Fortune Favors the Brave,* 9.

5. 1st Lt. R. B. Firm, Assistant R–2 (Intelligence Officer), 5th Marines to Major Guy Richards, 1st Marine Division, n.d. (but from text it appears to be April 1943, shortly after the 1st Marine Division's

movement to Australia from Guadalcanal), Regimental Intelligence, 62A-2086, Box 20, "Reconnaissance," 2–3, World War II, History and Museums Division, HQMC. This is a lengthy (fifteen pages) and pricelessly descriptive letter.

6. Ibid., 8.

Chapter 5. The Solomon Islands

1. Morison, *History* 5:4–5.
2. Richard B. Frank, *Guadalcanal: The Definitive Account of the Landmark Battle* (New York: Penguin Books, 1990), 48–50.
3. Morison, *History* 5:12–13, 4:264–66; Frank, *Guadalcanal.*
4. Morison, *History* 5:69; Lt. Col. Frank O. Hough, *History of Marine Corps Operations in World War II* (Washington, D.C.: Historical Branch, G-3 Division, HQMC), 1:281. (With the death of Lieutenant Colonel Goettge, the new G-2 appointed was Lt. Col. E. J. Buckley of the 11th Marines.)
5. Peter B. Mersky, *U.S. Marine Corps Aviation: 1912 to Present,* 3d ed. (Baltimore: Nautical and Aviation Publishing, 1997), 37, 44.
6. The bulk of the above report on Platoon Sergeant Pettus's patrol is taken from his excellent and very descriptive article "A Four-Day Patrol," *Marine Corps Gazette* 28, no. 6 (June 1944): 28–32. Additionally, this patrol was described in Joseph H. Alexander's book *Edson's Raiders* (Annapolis: Naval Institute Press, 2000), 212.
7. I brought two pair of the British jungle boots back to the United States and was briefing our commandant, Gen. David M. Shoup, and his staff at HQMC on the Malaya jungle patrols. General Shoup was swayed by my criticism of the U. S. footgear. He reached over and took the pair of British boots from me and handed them to the quartermaster general sitting next to him. Turning to the quartermaster, Shoup directed him to send my jungle boots to the Army development labs at Natick, Massachusetts. I was later advised that our now–standard U.S. jungle boots were "reverse engineered" and adapted from the pair brought back from the Gurkha patrols in Malaya to an even better jungle boot. The "new" American jungle boot added a steel shank for protection against punji sticks used in Vietnam.
8. Alexander, *Edson's Raiders.*
9. Frank, *Guadalcanal,* 263–64, 348, 352, 411, 413, 416, 418.
10. Hough, *History of Marine Corps Operations* 1:359–60.
11. John T. Hoffman, *Marine Raiders in the Pacific War,* historical monograph (Washington, D.C.: Historical Division, HQMC, 1995), 10.
12. Hough, *History of Marine Corps Operations* 1:261.

13. Smith and Finch, *Coral and Brass,* 104.
14. Morison, *History* 6:372–74.
15. See ibid., chap. 4, pp. 33–34; Frank and Shaw, *History* 2:301–4.
16. Hoffman, *Marine Raiders,* 26, and author interviews with Lieutenant Colonel Boyd while both of us were stationed at HQMC in July 1961 and Camp Lejeune in 1964.
17. Coleman, "Amphibious Recon Patrols," 23; also Hoffman, *Marine Raiders,* 27.
18. Hoffman, *Marine Raiders,* 26; Alexander, *Edson's Raiders,* 244, 247–46.
19. Tolbert, "Advance Man," 3–5, 4; Alexander, *Edson's Raiders,* 248–50.
20. Interviews with Boyd.
21. Coleman, "Amphibious Recon Patrols," 23.
22. Hoffman, *Marine Raiders,* 23–31; Morison, *History* 6:293–96; Coleman, "Amphibious Recon Patrols," 23–24; Commander Submarine Force, U.S. Pacific Fleet, "Submarine Operational History, World War II," 4 unpublished vols., World War II, Naval War College Archives, Newport, R.I. (hereafter cited as "Submarine History," followed by volume and page numbers), 2:983; Commander Landing Craft, 3d Amphibious Force, post-action report, "Treasury Island Occupation-October 1943," n.d., 2–3.
23. Coleman, "Amphibious Recon Patrols," 14.
24. Ibid., 25.
25. Morison, *History* 6:296; Carl W. Hoffman, *Silk Chutes and Hard Fighting: U.S. Marine Corps Parachute Units in World War II* (Washington, D.C.: History and Museum Division, HQMC, 1999), 24 n. 27.
26. "Submarine History" 2:860, 978; Morison, *History* 6:281.
27. "Submarine History" 2:980.
28. Morison, *History* 6:293–94, 289; Coleman, "Amphibious Recon Patrols," 13.
29. Coleman, "Amphibious Recon Patrols," 14.
30. Morison, *History* 6:283.
31. Ibid. 6:284–93; Coleman, "Amphibious Recon Patrols," 13–14; "Submarine History" 2:ii-983.
32. Morison, *History* 6:284, 290.
33. Ibid., 6:300.
34. Ibid.
35. Meyers, *Fortune Favors the Brave,* 1–3; McMillan, "Scouting at Cape Gloucester," *Marine Corps Gazette* 30, no. 5 (May 1946): 24–27.
36. Morison, *History* 6:370; Hoffman, *Silk Chutes,* 24–27.
37. Lt. Paul T. Relnner, USNR, became CO of MTB 21 and began operating from Seadler Harbor in the Admiralties two months later. Morison, *History* 6:446.

Chapter 6. The Gilbert Islands

1. Smith and Finch, *Coral and Brass,* 234.
2. Morison, *History* 7:76.
3. Frank and Shaw, *History* 3:50–51.
4. Morison, *History* 7:77; Smith and Finch, *Coral and Brass,* 132.
5. Frank and Shaw, *History* 7:23–25; Morison, *History* 7:86.
6. Chief of Naval Operations *Dictionary of American Fighting Ships* 5:28.
7. Keith Wheeler, *War Under the Pacific* (Alexandria, Va.: Time-Life Books, 1998), 134; Frank and Shaw, *History* 3:29; "Submarine History" 3:iii-1257–60.
8. Alexander, *Across the Reef;* Frank and Shaw, *History* 3:57.
9. Frank and Shaw, *History* 3:97.
10. Frank and Shaw, *History* 3:100; Morison, *History* 7:179–80.
11. Morison, *History* 7:179.
12. Capt. Charles E. Patrick, original member of Observer Group, interviews with author, Force Reconnaissance Association Reunions, San Antonio, 24 September 1999 and Louisville, Kentucky, 21 September 2001.
13. Gy. Sgt. Sam Lanford, interview with author, 7 June 1986, San Antonio, Texas. Adm. William D. Irwin, "Trials of the Nautilus," in *The Pacific War Remembered: An Oral History Collection,* ed. John T. Mason Jr. (Annapolis: Naval Institute Press, 1986), 182–83.
14. Ibid.
15. Ibid., 183.
16. *Nautilus* log, Patrol Seven, 19 November 1943, Submarine Patrol Log Files, Navy History Division, Washington Navy Yard, Washington, D.C.; also see Smith and Finch, *Coral and Brass,* 234; "Submarine History" 3:iii-1259.
17. Lanford interview.
18. Capt. James R. Stockman, *The Battle for Tarawa,* historical monograph (Washington, D.C. History and Museums Division, HQMC, 1947), 63; Smith and Finch, *Coral and Brass,* 234.
19. Stockman, *Tarawa,* 30; Frank and Shaw, *History* 3:57, 100–101.
20. Corey telephone interviews; Corey to author; Francis X. Tolbert, "Apamama: A Model Operation in Miniature," *Leatherneck* 28:2 (February 1945): 26–27; Brig. Gen. Russell E. Corey, "War Diary" (Apamama), Annex J, 3, History and Museums Division, HQMC.
21. Tolbert, "Apamama," 27.
22. Irwin, "Trials of the Nautilus," 187; Frank and Shaw, *History* 3:100–101; Morison, *History* 7:181.
23. Tolbert, "Apamama," 27.
24. Frank and Shaw, *History* 3:101–2.

25. Copy of Legion of Merit Medal citation, Medals and Decorations Branch, HQMC; copy in author's files.

Chapter 7. The Marshall Islands

1. Morison, *History* 7:201–7; Frank and Shaw, *History* 2:117–31.
2. "Submarine History" 2:ii-985–87.
3. Morison, *History* 7:207–8; Frank and Shaw, *History* 3:129.
4. Frank and Shaw, *History* 3:127.
5. Ibid. 3:127–29.
6. Col. Wallace M. Greene Jr. to CMC, 23 November 1952, cited in Frank and Shaw, *History* 3:122.
7. Sgt. Francis X. Tolbert, "The 'Recon Boys' at Majuro," *Leatherneck* 2, no. 11 (1 June 1946): 14–15; and Morison, *History* 7:226–27.
8. *Nautilus* log, Patrol Seven, 24 November 1943; Amphibious Reconnaissance Company, VAC, report, "War Diary, Operation of Reconnaissance Company on Sundance (Majuro)," 16 March 1944, Box 2, Folder A-19-10-VAC, OpnRept (encl. I), Recon Co. Report, 21 January–2 February 1944, History and Museums Division, HQMC.
9. Tolbert, "Recon Boys," 15.
10. Ibid; and 1st Lt. Harvey Weeks, "War Diary of 1st Lt.. Harvey Weeks," 6, Annex H of "War Diary, Operation of Amphib Recon Company on Sundance Atoll," 65A-5188, Box 2, Folder A-19-10-VAC, OpnRept (encl. I), Recon Co. Report, 21 January–2 February 1944, History and Museums Division, HQMC.
11. Tolbert, *Recon Boys,* 15.
12. Ibid.
13. Frank and Shaw, *History* 2:168; Morison, *History* 7:291.
14. Morison, *History* 7:291; Frank and Shaw, *History* 3:146, and photo, 127.
15. Frank and Shaw, *History* 3:151.
16. Ibid. 3:153.
17. Ibid. 3:154.
18. Ibid. 3:187.
19. Ibid. 3:185.
20. James Logan Jones Sr., "After-Action Report of the Amphibious Reconnaissance Company, Fifth Amphibious Corps, Downside (Catchpole) Operation," 9 March 1944, 1–9, secret declassified to unclassified; Frank and Shaw, *History* 3:195–204; Morison, *History* 7:291.
21. Jones, "After-Action Report," 4.
22. Lt. Gen. Thomas E. Watson to CMC, 1 March 1953, 3 April 1954, Historical Branch, G-3, HQMC.
23. Col. Edward L. Katzenbach Jr. to Head, 25 September 1962, Historical Branch, G-3, HQMC. (I worked closely with then–

Deputy Assistant Secretary of Defense Katzenbach in 1962–63, while I was serving as deputy assistant secretary of defense [manpower/personnel] in Secretary Robert McNamara's Office of the Secretary of Defense at the Pentagon.)

24. Jones, "After-Action Report," 6.
25. Ibid.
26. Frank and Shaw, *History* 3:208–9.
27. Ibid. 3:214–15.
28. Jones, "After-Action Report," 8–9.

Chapter 8. The Marianas

1. Table of Organization E-333, "Amphibious Reconnaissance Battalion, Amphibious Corps," 28 April 1944, copy at History and Museums Division, HQMC; former PFC Nelson Donley, telephone interview with author, 18 May 2002.
2. Melson and Hanon, *Marine Recon, 1940–1990,* 7.
3. Meyers, *Fortune Favors the Brave,* 3–4.
4. Smith and Finch, *Coral and Brass,* 181; Frank and Shaw, *History* 3:346.
5. Smith and Finch, *Coral and Brass,* 181.
6. Frank and Shaw, *History* 3:254, 263.
7. Ibid. 3:246; Morison, *History* 8:168.
8. Frank and Shaw, *History* 3:254–55.
9. Joseph H. Alexander, *Storm Landings: Epic Amphibious Battles in the Central Pacific* (Annapolis: Naval Institute Press, 1997), 71; Frank and Shaw, *History* 3:254–55; Morison, *History* 8:183–84, 374.
10. Nelson Donley, unpublished chronology of VAC Amphib Recon Battalion during World War II, Donley diary, 2, Donley Papers, copy in author's files (hereafter cited as Donley diary).
11. Former PFC Nelson Donley, telephone interview with author, 18 May 2002.
12. Frank and Shaw, *History* 3:306–21.
13. Ibid., 3:346; Morison, *History* 8:339.
14. Smith and Finch, *Coral and Brass,* 205; Frank and Shaw, *History* 3:374–75.
15. Smith and Finch, *Coral and Brass,* 207; Frank and Shaw, *History* 3:375.
16. Smith and Finch, *Coral and Brass,* 205.
17. Northern Troops and Landing Force Operation Order 27-44, 9 July 1944, Recon Files, History and Museums Division, HQMC. Top secret declassified to unclassified.
18. Ibid., 2.
19. Frank and Shaw, *History* 3:367–69.
20. Lanford interview; former PFC John Sebern, interview with author, 26 May 2003.

21. Col. Merwyn H. Silverthorn, USMC (Ret.) to author, 3 November 1996.

22. Ibid.; Frank and Shaw, *History* 3:367–70.

23. Frank and Shaw, *History* 3:421–22.

24. Ibid. 3:432–35.

25. Ibid. 3:436; Smith and Finch, *Coral and Brass,* 213.

26. Smith and Finch, *Coral and Brass,* 213–14; *Submarine Report* 2:ii-988.

27. Cyril J. O'Brien, *Liberation: Marines in the Recapture of Guam,* historical monograph (Washington, D.C.: Marine Corps Historical Center, 1994), 2; United States Fleet, "Invasion of the Marianas," chap. 4, p. 4-1.

28. Smith and Finch, *Coral and Brass,* 214.

29. Morison, *History* 8:379–80; United States Fleet, "Invasion of the Marianas," p. 4-1; O'Brien, "Liberation," 2.

30. O'Brien, "Liberation," 2; Morison, *History* 8:380; Frank and Shaw, *History* 3:441.

31. O'Brien, "Liberation," 18; Frank and Shaw, *History* 3:493–501; Morison, *History* 8:395.

32. 1st Lt. Robert Aurthur, USMCR, and 1st Lt. Kenneth Cohlmia, USMCR, *The Third Marine Division,* ed. Lt. Col. Robert T. Vance, USMC (Washington, D.C.: Infantry Journal Press, 1948), 151; O'Brien, "Liberation," 18.

33. Aurthur and Cohlmia, *Third Marine Division,* 151; Frank and Shaw, *History* 3:512–14.

34. Aurthur and Cohlmia, *Third Marine Division,* 151; O'Brien, "Liberation," 36–37; Frank and Shaw, *History* 3:545–48.

Chapter 9. Peleliu and the Palaus

1. George W. Garand and Truman R. Strobridge, *Western Pacific Operations* (Washington, D.C.: History and Museums Division, HQMC, 1971), 4:51.

2. Alexander, *Storm Landings,* 108.

3. Garand and Strobridge, *Western Pacific Operations* 4:52.

4. Alexander, *Storm Landings,* 108; Garand and Strobridge, *Western Pacific Operations* 4:66–74.

5. Brig. Gen. Gordon D. Gayle, *Bloody Beaches: The Marines at Peleliu,* USMC monograph (Washington, D.C.: History and Museums Division, HQMC, 1996), 8–11; Garand and Strobridge, *Western Pacific Operations* 4:67–68.

6. Alexander, *Storm Landings,* 111.

7. Garand and Strobridge, *Western Pacific Operations* 4:55–59.

8. "Submarine History" 2:ii-989; Garand and Strobridge, *Western Pacific Operations* 4:63, 78.

9. "Submarine History" 2:ii-989; Garand and Strobridge, *Western Pacific Operations* 4:79.

10. Williams, "Amphibious Scouts and Raiders," 150–57.

11. Morison, *History* 12:33. Morison describes this landing by UDT as having been on "the night of 13 August." The description taken from the official *Submarine Operational History, World War II* at ii-823–24 sets this landing as having occurred on 11 August 1944, two days before Morison's date. On 14 August, *Burrfish* left Peleliu and Angaur for Yap, where it conducted two beach recons on 16–18 August. The first two were successful on the southern tip of Yap, and the beach was found suitable for all types of landing craft.

12. *Submarine Operations* 2:ii-824.

13. Ibid. The three MIA UDT members were Chief Gunner's Mate Howard L. Reeder, QM1/c Robert A. Black, and SP(a)1/C John G. MacMahan, all USNR, Morison, *History* 12:33.

14. Garand and Strobridge, *Western Pacific Operations* 4:77–78.

15. Ibid. 4:65; Alexander, *Storm Landings*, 105–6.

16. Alexander, *Storm Landings*, 106; Morison, *History* 12:33.

17. Alexander, *Storm Landings*, 114–15.

18. Garand and Strobridge, *Western Pacific Operations* 4:130.

19. Ibid. 4:121–22, 130.

20. Ibid. 4:71; Morison, *History* 12:35–38.

21. Garand and Strobridge, *Western Pacific Operations* 4:131, 161; Gayle, *Bloody Beaches*, 48; Morison, *History* 12:41, 46; Alexander, *Storm Landings*, 124.

22. Garand and Strobridge, *Western Pacific Operations* 4:443–44; Alexander, *Storm Landings*, 124.

23. Alexander, *Storm Landings*, 124; Morison, *History* 12:43.

Chapter 10. The Volcano Islands and Iwo Jima

1. Garand and Strobridge, *Western Pacific Operations* 4:179; Morison, *History* 14:4–5.

2. Morison, *History* 14:4–7; Alexander, *Storm Landings*, 127.

3. Garand and Strobridge, *Western Pacific Operations* 4:450–51; Morison, *History* 14:14.

4. Garand and Strobridge, *Western Pacific Operations* 4:453–54; Morison, *History* 14:13–14; Alexander, *Storm Landings*, 131.

5. Garand and Strobridge, *Western Pacific Operations* 4:468, 483.

6. Smith and Finch, *Coral and Brass*, 243–44; Alexander, *Storm Landings*, 134–35; Garand and Strobridge, *Western Pacific Operations* 4:487–92, 492 n. 26.

7. Garand and Strobridge, *Western Pacific Operations* 4:486–87.

8. *Submarine Operations* 2:ii-993; Alexander, *Storm Landings*, 128.

9. Brig. Gen. Russell Corey, telephone interview with author, 10 June 2002.

10. From a description of UDT's Iwo activities by Motorman Charles Q. Lewis in *Navy Seals: A History* (Garden City, N.Y.: Dockery Military Book Club), pt. 1, p. 126.

   Just prior to publication of this book, I had the unique good fortune to be able to interview two former sergeants of the recon company of the 5th Marine Division. They provided the details of how these pre–D-day beach recons were actually done on Iwo Jima. Their ten-man recon team (six swimmers and three photographers) was led by their skipper, Capt. Robert C. Reynolds, USMC. Both sergeants interviewed participated as "recon photographers" in the D-2 recons of Iwo's beaches.

11. Former sergeant Jim Burns, USMC, telephone interviews with author, 20, 22 September, 5, 14 October 2003; and former sergeant Clete Peacock, telephone interview with author, 6 October 2003.

12. Dockery, *Navy Seals,* 136.

13. Morison, *History* 14:27–30.

14. Burns telephone interviews, and reference to copy of Sergeant Burns's Bronze Star Medal citation in author's files.

15. "Lighthouse," *Norfolk Virginian-Pilot,* 18 February 1968. (Sgt. Jim Burns returned to resume his newspaper photography with the *Albany Times-Union,* and Sgt. Pete Cletus became state editor of the *Virginian-Pilot.*)

16. Garand and Strobridge, *Western Pacific Operations* 4:496–500.

17. Brig. Gen. Russell Corey, interview with author, 10 June 2002, and Corey to author; Morison, *History* 14:31–32; Dockery, *Navy Seals,* 136–41.

18. Corey interview, 10 June 2002.

19. Ibid.

20. Ibid.; Morison, *History* 14:65.

21. Garand and Strobridge, *Western Pacific Operations* 4:698.

22. Ibid. 4:710; Corey interview, 10 June 2002; unpublished chronology of VAC Amphib Recon Battalion during World War II, Donley Papers; Morison, *History* 14:67.

Chapter 11. The Ryukyu Islands and Okinawa

1. Frank, *Guadalcanal* 5:31–36; Alexander, *Storm Landings,* 149–50; 1st Lt. Bevan G. Cass, USMC, *History of the Sixth Marine Division* (Washington, D.C.: Infantry Journal Press, 1948), 40–43; Morison, *History* 14:79–83.

2. Alexander, *Storm Landings,* 149–52; Morison, *History* 14:156–98, 243–45.

3. Robert Leckie, *Okinawa: The Last Battle of World War II* (New York: Viking, 1995), 5; Joseph H. Alexander, *The Final Campaign: Marines in the Victory on Okinawa,* monograph (Washington, D.C.: History and Museums Division, HQMC), 2.

4. Frank, *Guadalcanal* 5:40–44; Alexander, *Storm Landings,* 152; Morison, *History* 14:101.

5. Alexander, *Final Campaign,* 21–22; Alexander, *Storm Landings,*152; Frank, *Guadalcanal* 5:99–100, 176, 186; Morison, *History* 14:89.

6. Morison, *History* 14:282; Alexander, *Storm Landings,* 164–65; Frank, *Guadalcanal* 5:99, 176, 186.

7. Morison, *History* 14:90–91; Alexander, *Storm Landings,*150; Frank, *Guadalcanal* 5:60.

8. Frank, *Guadalcanal* 5:60; Alexander, *Final Campaign,* 7; Alexander, *Storm Landings,* 159–60.

9. Morison, *History* 14:93, 103–4.

10. Frank, *Guadalcanal* 5:48–49.

11. Ibid. 5:61, 78–79.

12. Ibid. 5:80; *Submarine Operations* 2:ii-995; Morison, *History* 14:288–89.

13. Morison, *History* 14:276; Alexander, *Storm Landings,* 171; Frank, *Guadalcanal* 5:363.

14. Frank, *Guadalcanal* 5:393.

15. Donley diary, 2.

16. Ibid.; Alexander, *Final Campaign,* 49; Frank, *Guadalcanal* 5:64–66.

17. Frank, *Guadalcanal* 5:99, 104; Donley diary, 2.

18. Frank, *Guadalcanal* 5:106; Battalion Operation Order 1-45, March 1946. Amphib Recon Battalion, FMFPac, "Reconnaissance of Mae Shima and Kuro Shima, report on," 29 March 1945, Gray Research Center Archives, Marine Corps University, Quantico, Va. Formerly top secret, now unclassified.

19. Donley diary, 2; Frank, *Guadalcanal* 5:109; Alexander, *Final Campaign,* 12.

20. Frank, *Guadalcanal* 5:162; Morison, *History* 14:220.

21. Nelson Donley, unpublished account of Tsugen Shima Operation, in author's files.

22. Frank, *Guadalcanal* 5:163–64; Morison, *History* 14:221.

23. Ibid.

24. Morison, *History* 14:221.

25. Donley diary, 2; Frank, *Guadalcanal* 5:167.

26. Brig. Gen. Russ Corey, interview with author, 17 May 2003; Thomas Martin, professor of toxicology, University of Washington (UW) Medical School, interview with author, 4 June 2003; Ray Huey, UW professor of zoology, 4 June 2003, re: methodology of antivenom

production from injection of venom into horses; Cass, *History of the Sixth Marine Division,* 40.

27. Author interview with Col. Tony "Cold Steel" Walker of 13 June 2002. Research of the sobriquet "Cold Steel" was traced to his instructing in bayonet and knife fighting.
28. Frank, *Guadalcanal* 5:125–27; also Col. Edward W. Snedeker to CMC, 27 March 1947, cited in Frank, *Guadalcanal* 5:127 n. 31.
29. Frank, *Guadalcanal* 5:134.
30. Cass, *History of the Sixth Marine Division,* 60.
31. Frank, *Guadalcanal* 5:140; Cass, *History of the Sixth Marine Division,* 56–57.
32. Cass, *History of the Sixth Marine Division,* 76.
33. Alexander, *Storm Landings,* 165; Cass, *History of the Sixth Marine Division,* 76; Frank, *Guadalcanal* 5:196.
34. Alexander, *Storm Landings;* Frank, *Guadalcanal* 5:196.
35. Frank, *Guadalcanal* 5:247.
36. Ibid. 5:276, 283–84.
37. Ibid. 5:302–5; Cass, *History of the Sixth Marine Division,* 145; Alexander, *Storm Landings,* 169.
38. Alexander, *Storm Landings,* 169; Cass, *History of the Sixth Marine Division,* 145; Frank, *Guadalcanal* 5:302–3.
39. Frank, *Guadalcanal* 5:302; Alexander, *Storm Landings,* 169.
40. Alexander, *Storm Landings,* 169; Cass, *History of the Sixth Marine Division,* 145–55; Frank, *Guadalcanal* 5:304–5.
41. Donley diary, 3; Frank, *Guadalcanal* 5:348–49, map.
42. Ibid.
43. Frank, *Guadalcanal* 5:323–24.
44. Ibid. 5:347–48.
45. Ibid.
46. Ibid. 5:378 n. 52.

Epilogue

1. Donley diary, 2.
2. Frank, *Guadalcanal* 5:449–64.
3. Ibid. 5:435; Morison, *History* 14:351.
4. Frank, *Guadalcanal* 5:438; Morison, *History* 14:357.
5. Morison, *History* 14:355; Frank, *Guadalcanal* 5:543–52.
6. Frank, *Guadalcanal* 5:476, map.
7. Cass, *History of the Sixth Marine Division,* 226.
8. Frank, *Guadalcanal* 5:468.
9. Ibid. 5:512.
10. Ibid. 5:516, 650.
11. Ibid. 5:469.

12. Ibid. 5:470.
13. Philip N. Pierce and Frank Hough, *The Compact History Of the United States Marine Corps* (New York: Hawthorn Books, 1960), 279–80; Brig. Gen. Edward Simmons, "The Marines," 10; Simmons, "The United States Marines: The First Two Hundred Years, 1775–1975," 253.
14. Melson and Hanon, *Marine Recon, 1940–1990,* 9–10.
15. Author's interviews with Lieutenant Colonel Fuller from 1954 to 1957.
16. Meyers, *Fortune Favors the Brave,* 23–36.
17. Ibid., 127.
18. Ibid., 135–46.
19. Ibid., 159–62.
20. Ibid., 165–70.
21. Headquarters Marine Corps, MarAdmin Bulletin 292/99, History and Museums Division, HQMC; also see Stephen Cala, *Marine Corps Times,* 19 July 1999, p. 18.

Bibliography

Primary and Secondary Sources

Alexander, Joseph H. *Across the Reef: The Marine Assault of Tarawa.* Historical monograph. Washington, D.C.: History and Museums Division, HQMC, 1993.

———. *Edson's Raiders.* Annapolis: Naval Institute Press, 2000.

———. *The Final Campaign: Marines in the Victory on Okinawa.* Historical monograph. Washington, D.C.: History and Museums Division, HQMC, 1996.

———. *Storm Landings: Epic Amphibious Battles in the Central Pacific.* Annapolis: Naval Institute Press, 1997.

Amphibious Corps, Pacific Fleet, Camp Elliot, San Diego, California. "Reconnaissance Patrols Landing on Hostile Shores." Intelligence Order 4-42, 29 October 1942, 62A 2086, Box 20, "Reconnaissance," World War II, History and Museum Division, HQMC, Washington, D.C.

Amphibious Reconnaissance Battalion, Corps Troops, VAC. "Report of Readiness," 30 June 1944. Annex D: Weapons, Marine Corps T/O E-333. History and Museum Division, HQMC, Washington, D.C.

Amphibious Reconnaissance Company, VAC. "Downside (Catchpole) Opn" (Eniwetok). History and Museum Division, HQMC, Washington, D.C. Secret declassified to unclassified.

———. "War Diary, Operation of Reconnaissance Company on Sundance (Majuro Atoll)." Report. 16 March 1944. History and Museums Division, HQMC, Washington, D.C.

Aurthur, 1st Lt. Robert A., USMCR, and 1st Lt. Kenneth Cohlmia, USMCR. *The Third Marine Division.* Edited by Lt. Col. Robert T. Vance, USMC. Washington D.C.: Infantry Journal Press, 1948.

Bartlett, Merrill L., and Dirk A. Ballendorf. *Pete Ellis: An Amphibious Warfare Prophet.* Annapolis: Naval Institute Press, 1996.

Buerline, Robert A. *Allied Military Fighting Knives and the Men Who Made Them Famous.* Richmond, Va.: American Historical Foundation, 1984.

Cain, Stephen. "'Best of Best' Wanted for Recon." *Marine Corps Times,* 19 July 1999, p. 18.

Cass, 1st Lt. Bevan G., USMC. *History of the Sixth Marine Division.* Washington, D.C.: Infantry Journal Press, 1948.

Chief of Naval Operations. *Dictionary of American Fighting Ships.* 7 vols. Washington, D.C.: GPO, 1968.

———. *Landing Operations Doctrine.* Washington, D.C.: GPO, 1938.

Coleman, William F. "Amphibious Reconnaissance Patrols." *Marine Corps Gazette* 29, no. 12 (December 1945): 22–25, and vol. 30, no. 1 (January 1946): 13–15.

Commander Fifth Amphibious Force to CinCPac. "Underwater Demolition Teams, Recommendations Concerning-Based on Experience in Flintlock" (Kwajalein). Report. 2 June 1944. Declassified from secret.

Commander Submarine Force, U.S. Pacific Fleet. "Submarine Operational History, World War II." 4 unpublished vols. World War II, Naval War College Archives, Newport, R.I. Initially classified as secret, declassified to unclassified.

——. "War Diary of 1st Lt. Russell Corey USMC, 3rd Platoon (Amphib Recon Co, VAC)." Annex J, "War Diary of Sundance Atoll (Apamama)." Corps Training Memorandum 25-44, 28 March 1944.

Davis, Burke. *Marine! The Life of Lt. Gen. Lewis B. ("Chesty") Puller.* Boston: Little, Brown, 1962.

Donley, Nelson. Unpublished chronology of Operations of Amphibious Reconnaissance Battalion, VAC, III AC, FMFPac, n.d. Copy in author's files.

Frank, Benis M., and Henry I. Shaw Jr. *Victory and Occupation.* Vol. 5 of *History of U.S. Marine Corps Operations in World War II.* Washington, D.C.: Historical Branch, G-3 Division, HQMC, 1968.

Frank, Richard B. *Guadalcanal: The Definitive Account of the Landmark Battle.* New York: Penguin Books, 1990.

Garand, George W., and Truman R. Strobridge. *Western Pacific Operations,* vol. 4. Washington, D.C.: Historical Division, HQMC, 1971.

Gayle, Brig. Gen. Gordon D. "Bloody Beaches: The Marines at Peleliu." USMC monograph. Washington, D.C.: History and Museums Division, HQMC, 1996.

Harwood, Richard. *A Close Encounter: The Marine Landing on Tinian.* Historical monograph. Washington, D.C.: History and Museums Division, HQMC, 1994.

Headquarters Marine Corps. MarAdmin Bulletin 292/99. History and Museum Division, HQMC, Washington, D.C.

Headquarters V Amphibious Corps. "Reconnaissance Patrols Landing on Hostile Shores." Corps Training Memorandum No. 25-44, 25 March 1944. Confidential (now declassified). Box 62A 2086, Box 20, "Reconnaissance," World War II, Historical Archives, HQMC, Washington, D.C.

Hoffman, Carl W. *The Seizure of Tinian.* Historical monograph. Washington, D.C.: Historical Division, HQMC, 1951.

Hoffman, John T. *Marine Raiders in the Pacific War.* Historical monograph. Washington, D.C.: Historical Division, HQMC, 1995.

———. *Once a Legend: "Red Mike" Edson of the Marine Raiders.* Novato, Calif.: Presidio Press, 1994,

———. *Silk Chutes and Hard Fighting: U.S. Marine Corps Parachute Units in World War II.* Washington, D.C.: History and Museum Division, HQMC, 1999.

Hough, Lt. Col. Frank O. *History of U.S. Marine Corps Operations in World War II.* Vol. 1, *Pearl Harbor to Guadalcanal.* Washington, D.C.: Historical Branch, G-3 Division, HQMC.

Irvin, Rear Adm. William D., USN (Ret.). "Trials of the Nautilus." In *The Pacific War Remembered: An Oral History Collection,* ed., John T. Mason Jr. Annapolis, Md.: Naval Institute Press, 1986. Copy in author's files received from Charlotte Jones from the papers of Maj. James Jones.

Jones, James Logan, Sr. "After-Action Report of the Amphibious Reconnaissance Company, Fifth Amphibious Corps, Downside (Catchpole)," 9 March 1944, secret declassified to unclassified, and V MAC Amph Rcn Co., Ready Report, March 1944, 65A-5049, Box 88, History and Museums Division, HQMC; Amphibious Reconnaissance Company, VAC report, "War Diary, Operation of Reconnaissance Company on Sundance (Majuro)," 16 March 1944, secret declassified to unclassified, and Recon Company report, January–2 February 1944, 65A-5188, Box 2, Folder A-19-10-VAC, Opn Rpt (encl. I), History and Museums Division, HQMC.

———. "Report of Readiness, Amphibious Reconnaissance Battalion, VAC Corps Troops," 30 June 1944, 25. Copy in author's files. Washington, D.C.: Marine Corps Historical Files, File V, MAC, Amph Rcn Bn., April–June 1944, 65A-5099, Box 88. Initially classified secret, now declassified.

Lanning, Michael Lee, with Ray William Stubbe. *Inside Force Recon: Recon Marines in Vietnam.* New York: Ivy Books, 1989.

Leckie, Robert. *Okinawa: The Last Battle of World War II.* New York: Penguin, Viking, 1995.

Lee, Lt. Col. Alex. *Force Recon Command.* Annapolis: Naval Institute Press, 1995.

Marquis, Susan L. *Unconventional Warfare: Rebuilding U.S. Special Operations Forces.* Washington, D.C.: Brookings Institution, 1997.

McKelvy, W. H., Jr. CO Company F, 2d Battalion, 5th Marines. "Report of Operations during Puerto Rico Campaign, 2–3Mar38." 4 February 1938. And enclosure I, "Attack Force Order of 2Feb38," to Commander, U.S. Fleet Training Detachment, USS *New York.*

McMillan, George. "Scouting at Cape Gloucester." *Marine Corps Gazette* 30, no. 5 (May 1946): 24–27.

Melson, Charles D. "Recon Marines: Amphibious and Ground Reconnaissance Units." Unpublished monograph, Washington, D.C.: Historical Branch, G-3 Division, HQMC.

Melson, Charles D., and Paul Hanon. *Marine Recon, 1940–1990.* Elite series, no. 55. London: Osprey, 1998.

Mersky, Peter B. *U.S. Marine Corps Aviation: 1900 to Present.* 3d ed. Baltimore: Nautical & Aviation Publishing, 1997.

Meyers, Bruce F. "Force Recon." *Marine Corps Gazette* 45, no. 5 (May 1961): 48–53.

———. *Fortune Favors the Brave: The Story of First Force Recon.* Annapolis: Naval Institute Press, 2000,

———. "Jungle Canopy Operations." *Marine Corps Gazette* 53, no. 7 (July 1969): 20–26.

———. "Malaya Jungle Patrols." *Marine Corps Gazette* 44, no. 10 (October 1960): 28–35.

Morison, Samuel Eliot. *History of United States Naval Operations in World War II.* Vol. 2, *Operations in North African Waters: October 1942–June 1943;* vol. 5, *The Struggle for Guadalcanal: August 1942–February 1943;* vol. 6, *Breaking the Bismarck's Barrier: 22 July 1942–1 May 1944;* vol. 7, *Aleutians, Gilberts and Marshalls: June 1942–April 1944;* vol. 8, *New Guinea and the Marianas: March 1944–August 1944.* vol. 12, *Leyte: June 1944–January 1945;* vol. 14, *Victory in the Pacific, 1945;* and vol. 15, *Supplement and General Index.* Edison, N.J.: Castle Books, 2001.

Northern Troops and Landing Force Operation Order 27-44. 9 July 1944 (TINIAN). Originally classified top secret, now declassified to unclassified. Includes Annex ABLE "Signal Communications." Copy in author's files. Received from Nelson Donley.

Norton, Maj. Bruce H. *Force Recon Diary, 1969.* New York: Random House, Bantam Books, 1991.

O'Brien, Cyril J. *Liberation: Marines in the Recapture of Guam.* Historical monograph. Washington, D.C.: Marine Corps Historical Center, 1994.

Pettus, Plt. Sgt. Francis C. "A Four-Day Patrol." *Marine Corps Gazette* 28, no. 6 (June 1944): 28–32.

Pierce, Philip N., and Frank Hough. *The Compact History Of the United States Marine Corps.* New York: Hawthorn Books, 1960.

Roscoe, Theodore. *United States Submarine Operations in World War II.* Annapolis: Naval Institute Press, 1949.

Rottman, Gordon. *U.S. Marine Corps, 1941–45.* Military Book Club edition. London: Osprey, 1998.

——. *U.S. Marine Corps World War II Order of Battle: Ground and Air Units in the Pacific War, 1939–1945.* Military Book Club edition. Westport, Conn.: Greenwood Press, 2002.

Shaw, Henry I., Jr., and Maj. Douglas T. Kane, USMC. *Isolation of Rabaul.* Vol. 2 of *History of U.S. Marine Corps Operations in World War II.* Washington, D.C.: Historical Branch, G-3 Division, HQMC, 1963.

Shaw, Henry I. Jr., Bernard C. Nalty, Edwin T. Turnbladh, *Central Pacific Drive.* Vol. 3 of *History of U.S. Marine Corps Operations in World War II.* Washington, D.C.: Historical Branch, G-3 Division, HQMC, 1966.

Shinn, Leo B. "Amphibious Reconnaissance." *Marine Corps Gazette* 29, no. 4 (April 1945): 50–51.

Simmons, Brig. Gen. Edward H. *The Marines.* Quantico, Va.: Marine Corps Heritage Foundation, 1998.

——. *The United States Marines: First Two Hundred Years.* New York: Viking, 1974, 1976.

Smith, Gen. Holland M. "The Development of Amphibious Tactics in the U.S. Navy." *Marine Corps Gazette* 30, no. 9 (October 1946): 43–47.

Smith, Gen. Holland M., and Perry Finch. *Coral and Brass.* New York: Scribner's, 1949.

Steinberg, Rafael. *Island Fighting, World War II.* Collector's edition. New York: Time-Life Books, 1978.

Stockman, Capt. James R. *The Battle for Tarawa.* Historical monograph. Washington, D.C.: Historical Division, HQMC, 1947.

Tolbert, Francis X. "The Advance Man." *Leatherneck* 2, no. 5 (March 1945): 3–5.

——. "Apamama: A Model Operation in Miniature," *Leatherneck* 28, no. 2 (February 1945): 26–27 .

——. "The `Recon Boys' at Majuro." *Leatherneck* 11 (1 June 1945): 14–15.

United States Fleet. Headquarters of Commander in Chief. "Invasion of the Marianas, June to August 1944." COMINCH P-007. Report. Navy History Division, Washington, D.C. Declassified from secret. N.d. Chap. 4, "Ship to Shore Movement," pp. 41, 126.

Weeks, 1st. Lt. Harvey, USMCR. "War Diary of 1st Lt. Harvey Weeks." Annex H of War Diary, Operation of Amphib Recon Company on Sundance Atoll (Apamama). Copy at Archives, Marine Corps University, Quantico, Va. Declassified from secret.

Wheeler, Keith. *War Under the Pacific.* Alexandria, Va.: Time-Life Books, 1998, 134.

Williams, Ralph Chester. "Amphibious Scouts and Raiders." *Military Affairs* 13, no. 3 (1949): 150–57.

Zedric, Larry Q. *Silent Warriors of World War II: The Alamo Scouts Behind Japanese Lines.* Ventura, Calif.: Pathfinder Publications, 1995.

Zimmerman, J. L. "Island Coastwatchers." *Marine Corps Gazette* 30, no. 1 (January 1946): 16–18.

Interviews with the Author

Boyd, Col. Clay, USMC (Ret.). HQMC, Washington, D.C., July 1961; Camp Lejeune, N.C., summer 1964.

Burns, Sgt. Jim, USMC (Ret.) Telephone interviews, 20, 22 September and 5, 14 October 2003.

Corey, Brig. Gen. Russell E., USMC (Ret.). Telephone interviews, 10, 15 June, 17 July 2002, and 17 May 2003; Quantico, Va., August 2002.

Donley, Nelson. Telephone interviews, 18 May 2002 and 8 June 2003.

Fuller, Brig. Gen. Regan, USMC (Ret.). Camp Pendleton, Calif., April 1954, May 1957.

Huey, Prof. Raymond. Telephone interview, 3 June 2003. Re: antivenom production for Habu snakes.

Lanford, Gy. Sgt. Samuel, USMC (Ret.). San Antonio, Texas, 7 June 1986.

Martin, Prof. Thomas. Telephone interview, 4 June 2003. Re: Habu poisonous snakes.

Patrick, Capt. Charles E., USMC (Ret.). Force Reconnaissance Association Reunions, 3 June 2002; San Antonio, Texas, 24 September 1999; Louisville, Kentucky, 21 September 2001; 24 March 2002.

Peacock, Sgt. Clete, USMC. Telephone interview, 6 October 2003.

Sebern, John. Former PFC. 26 May 2003. Re: experience in recon of Yellow Beach on Tinian.

Silverthorn, Col. Merwyn H., USMC (Ret.). 6 May, 11 June 1997.

Walker, Col. Anthony, USMC (Ret). 13 June 2003. Re: command of Recon Co., 6th Marine Division during World War II.

Index

About the Author

Bruce F. Meyers, born and raised in Seattle, Washington, joined the U.S. Navy in 1943 at the age of seventeen. Serving at sea in World War II as a midshipman in the Pacific, he was commissioned in 1945 as a marine second lieutenant and given command of a combat swimming platoon. After service in Korea as a rifle company commander in the 5th Marines, he returned to the States as officer in charge of the Amphibious Reconnaissance School at Coronado, California. Meyers trained as a parachutist and diver; later, having attained the rank of Marine Corps major, he formed and became the first commanding officer of 1st Force Recon Company.

After going on to serve with the 3d Marine Division on Okinawa, Meyers became landing force commander of the Sixth Fleet in the Mediterranean. Upon graduating from the Naval War College and arriving in Vietnam as a colonel, he initially commanded Special Landing Force Alpha on the USS *Iwo Jima* and later took command of the 26th Marine Regiment. Having completed twenty-eight years of service, he retired from the Marine Corps in 1970 and entered the practice of law as a trial attorney, later becoming an associate dean and an associate professor at a West Coast law school. He is also the author of *Fortune Favors the Brave: The Story of First Force Recon,* also published by the Naval Institute Press.

Meyers and his wife, Jo, reside in Seattle in the foothills of the Cascade Mountains. They have three sons.

About the Author

[illegible] D.C. [illegible] the age of seven [illegible] World War II and [illegible] joined [illegible] in 1948 [illegible] and of a [illegible] After [illegible]

[illegible] Mayes [illegible] and [illegible] of [illegible] became the [illegible] commanding officer of [illegible] Barracks.

After [illegible] with the 3d Marine Division [illegible] commanding officer [illegible] War College and [illegible] in Vietnam [illegible] commanded [illegible] Landing Team [illegible] and [illegible] commanded [illegible] completed [illegible] with [illegible] on the [illegible] [illegible]

[illegible]

The Naval Institute Press is the book-publishing arm of the U.S. Naval Institute, a private, nonprofit, membership society for sea service professionals and others who share an interest in naval and maritime affairs. Established in 1873 at the U.S. Naval Academy in Annapolis, Maryland, where its offices remain today, the Naval Institute has members worldwide.

Members of the Naval Institute support the education programs of the society and receive the influential monthly magazine *Proceedings* and discounts on fine nautical prints and on ship and aircraft photos. They also have access to the transcripts of the Institute's Oral History Program and get discounted admission to any of the Institute-sponsored seminars offered around the country.

The Naval Institute also publishes *Naval History* magazine. This colorful bimonthly is filled with entertaining and thought-provoking articles, first-person reminiscences, and dramatic art and photography. Members receive a discount on *Naval History* subscriptions.

The Naval Institute's book-publishing program, begun in 1898 with basic guides to naval practices, has broadened its scope to include books of more general interest. Now the Naval Institute Press publishes about one hundred titles each year, ranging from how-to books on boating and navigation to battle histories, biographies, ship and aircraft guides, and novels. Institute members receive significant discounts on the Press's more than eight hundred books in print.

Full-time students are eligible for special half-price membership rates. Life memberships are also available.

For a free catalog describing Naval Institute Press books currently available, and for further information about subscribing to *Naval History* magazine or about joining the U.S. Naval Institute, please write to:

Membership Department
U.S. Naval Institute
291 Wood Road
Annapolis, MD 21402-5034
Telephone: (800) 233-8764
Fax: (410) 269-7940
Web address: www.navalinstitute.org